TIMELESS ELEGANCE

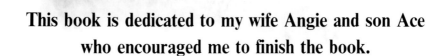

This book is dedicated to my wife Angie and son Ace who encouraged me to finish the book.

ACKNOWLEDGEMENTS

Many other people contributed to this endeavour — Alan Chan, Hong Kong; Brad Gold, L.A. Watch, L.A., California; David Lowe, Irvan, Hong Kong; David Mears Barclay's London, Tina Millar, Sotheby's, London; Ron Nassar New York; John Read, England; Bernard S. Roth, New York; Michael Szarvassy, New York; Osvaldo Patrizzi, Hapsburg Feldman, Geneva; Virginia Virtuose, New York; Dr. Bernard Wong, Treasure Island, Hong Kong; Musee International de H'orologie, Chaud de Fond, Switzerland.

Publisher
Alan Zie Yongder

Author
George Gordon

Art Director
Ellis Cheng

Production Manager
Zoo Shui Wo

For 'VINTAGE ROLEX WRISTWATCHES',
photography by courtesy of Sandy Lee and Tsai King Yan,
art direction by courtesy of Alan Chan and Anne Ma.

Distributor
Timekeepers International Ltd. (non-book store)
173 Coleherne Court, Redcliffe Gardens
London SW5, England
Tel.: 44-1-373-7807, FAX.: 44-1-373-0347
Dragonprint International Ltd. (book-store)
18/F, Java Centre, 128 Java Road
North Point, Hong Kong
Tel.: 5-626937 Fax: 5-655250

Published by Zie Yongder Co., Ltd.
G/F. Cheung Kong Building, 661 King's Road, Hong Kong
Tel: 5-651313 Fax: 5-658217

ISBN. 962-7359-01-7

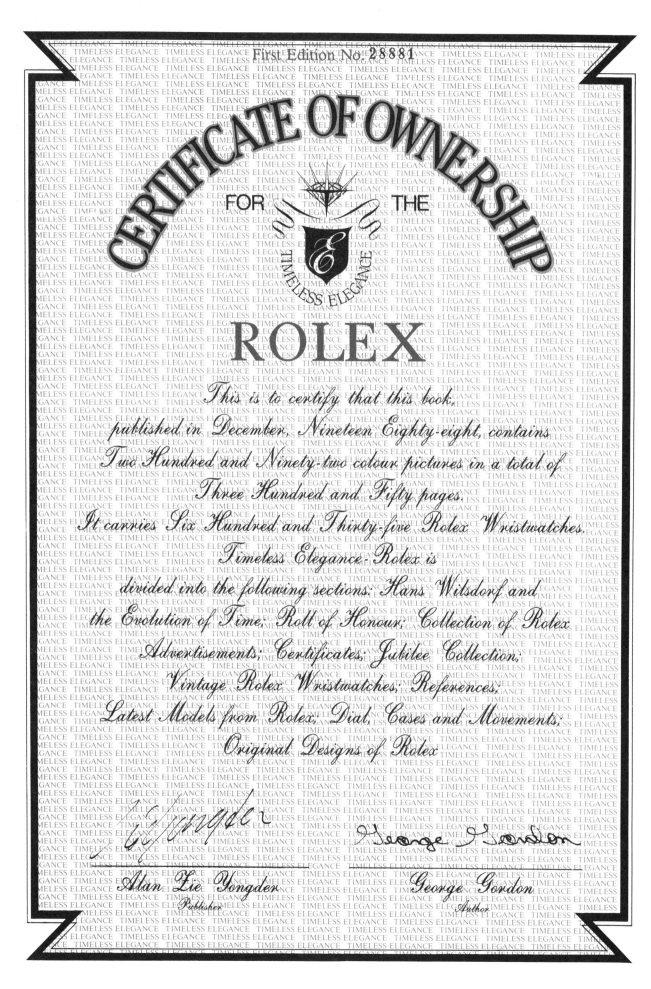

First Edition No: 28881

CERTIFICATE OF OWNERSHIP

FOR THE

ROLEX

This is to certify that this book,
published in December, Nineteen Eighty-eight, contains
Two Hundred and Ninety-two colour pictures in a total of
Three Hundred and Fifty pages.
It carries Six Hundred and Thirty-five Rolex Wristwatches.
Timeless Elegance - Rolex is
divided into the following sections: Hans Wilsdorf and
the Evolution of Time; Roll of Honour; Collection of Rolex
Advertisements; Certificates; Jubilee Collection;
Vintage Rolex Wristwatches; References;
Latest Models from Rolex; Dial, Cases and Movements;
Original Designs of Rolex

Alan Zie Yongder
Publisher

George Gordon
Author

INDEX

PREFACE

$\mathcal{T}$hroughout history, man has sought to improve the quality of watchmaking. Hans Wilsdorf's desire was to develop, manufacture, and market time itself. After the turn of the century, through his ability and determination, Rolex was started and became the most unusual company of its kind. By always giving the highest quality and craftsmanship in his products, he made them renowned for their excellence, style, dependability and value.

His dream was to expand Rolex to new horizons, always ready to meet the demands and make the improvements that the company stands for. Today, Rolex still believes in this philosophy. That is why it takes one year to produce a gold Rolex chronometer and the company is responsible for 25% of the total Swiss exports, marketed around the world. This is also why Rolex has become the best known wristwatch company in the world.

Wilsdorf's belief that the customer was entitled to the best service and quality became the basic principle behind Rolex and innovated unique ideas which kept him one step ahead of all the other manufacturers. The trademarks, the crown, shows this immediately for it represents the five fingers of the hand, in turn handmade.

The Observatory certificates awarded to Rolex Chronometers have attested to their perfection throughout the company's history. Wilsdorf's dream has been fulfilled and he will always be remembered. I hope this book is a lasting memorial to Hans Wilsdorf and his evolution of the Rolex Wristwatch.

George Gordon

ROLEX

1905-1989

HANS WILSDORF
AND THE EVOLUTION OF TIME

*C*raftsmanship, innovation and excellence. For the past eighty-four years, these ideals have been the trademark of the Rolex Watch Company. Dedicated from its inception to furthering the standards of the watchmaking industry, its timepieces remain coveted items of luxury, beauty and precision.

♛ "All my possessions for a moment of time," the last words spoken by Queen Elizabeth I of England could as well have been attributed to the young German, Hans Wilsdorf, who later became a British Subject founder of the Rolex Watch Company.

♛ Wilsdorf was nineteen years old when he first discovered the watchmaking industry. He was sent to work in Switzerland for an exporter of watches and clocks and became fascinated by the workings of these chronometers. Wilsdorf soon turned his attention to London, which was then the economic capital of the world due to its widespread colonies. And in 1905, using money borrowed from his brother-in-law and sister, founded with his brother-in-law a company which manufactured cases and distributed wristwatches, a case-manufacturing company, Wilsdorf & Davis.

♛ The economy was buoyant. Clock importers were doing a roaring trade but to Wilsdorf's critical eye, quality was greatly lacking. It was this constant striving for perfection that was to set Wilsdorf apart from his competitors and give Rolex the world acclaim that it has achieved today. Although the standards were perfectly acceptable to others in his profession, they fell short of his. Wilsdorf realised there was much room for improvement and he set about to ensure that, at least the watches and clocks sold by his company, were of a quality that satisfied his own ideas of perfection.

♛ It was about this time that the wrist watch was making its appearance. Until then the pocket watch had been king.

A fine pocket watch gave a man an air of respectability. At first, the public had viewed the new invention derisively. Gentlemen were heard to remark that they would sooner wear a skirt as wear a wrist watch! Horologists were also wary but from a more practical point of view. They felt that the mechanism required by a wrist watch would be too small to be accurate or to withstand the constant arm movement. They also felt that it would be impossible to make such a delicate movement resist the attacks of dust and dirt. In consequence, few firms were prepared to manufacture and sell wrist watches.

Wilsdorf viewed these obstacles as a challenge for he recognised that if he could overcome these problems, he would also be improving the standards of watch and clock making in general. He was proved right. This constant striving for smaller and more accurate movements, brought about by the arrival of the wristwatch, revolutionised the Swiss watchmaking industry since it forced watchmakers out of their complacency into re-examining their manufacturing procedures.

Wilsdorf & Davis had by now established itself as a firm specialising in unusual products. Hand in hand with Wilsdorf's search for quality went his search for originality. The company had already launched the portfolio watch and was also selling travelling clocks cased in top quality leather boxes. The wristwatch would be a welcome addition.

Wilsdorf developed and improved the small calibre in cooperation which the firm of Aegler in Bienne, Switzerland about whom he had heard during his years as an apprentice and who had now earned the reputation of making good quality lever escapement movements. They agreed to supply him with movements small enough to be worn on the wrist. This first order was a turning point since it represented a sum five times greater than that of the entire capital of Wilsdorf & Davis in the amount of several hundred thousand Swiss francs.

⚜ From then on, Wilsdorf made and sold watches: his cases with works imported from Bienne. Wilsdorf decided that the wristwatch should be available to the general public, affordable, stylish and accurate. One of the novelties of his production was the variety of case designs: sporty, casual, formal and others. His vision brought him to the forefront of the industry for the wristwatch became an accessory that no well dressed man or woman would be without. Soon people owned several wristwatches to be worn depending on their outfit or what they were doing. The wristwatch proved to be most popular among the sporting gentlemen of England.

⚜ All the parts that came to Wilsdorf originated from different places. Until then it had been the custom for the retailers name to appear not only on the dial but also on the movement. Wilsdorf realised that his own name would be advantageous in distinguishing his watches from those of his competitors, which he believed to be inferior since they did not have to undergo the exacting tests that his own had to. In 1908, the name Rolex was coined. It was chosen specifically because it was easily pronounceable in most European languages and because it was short enough to be written on a watch dial. Wilsdorf did not anticipate the battle he would be obliged to fight to have the name Rolex, and not that of the supplier, appear on his watches. Rolex movements also bore the names X/L, W/D, Marconi, Unicorn, Genex, Rolco, Oyster and Tudor.

⚜ In 1910, a Rolex movement was sent to the School of Horology at Bienne, which later became one of the official institutes of time keeping tests. It was judged excellent and was awarded a chronometer bulletin. This then was the world's first wrist chronometer combining the accuracy of a chronometer with the size of a small watch. No longer could these new timepieces be ignored.

⚜ A Rolex movement went on to receive another distinction when, in 1914, it was awarded a Class A Certificate by the Kew Observatory in Britain. This was the first wrist watch ever to receive the award as the tests, which were normally for large chronometers, made no allowances for the small wrist watch movements, which had to undergo five position tests and three temperature tests.

W The news startled the horological world. Wilsdorf decided that henceforth all Rolex timepieces should be submitted to similar tests carried out by impartial institutes. No Rolex chronometer would ever be sold again without its Official Timing Certificate. And today, for a timepiece to be sold as a chronometer, it is obligatory that it be accompanied by an Official Timing Certificate.

W After World War I, import tax was raised to 33% and Wilsdorf was forced to leave England for Switzerland. He left the London company in the hands of managers and moved to Geneva where, in 1919, he founded Montres Rolex S.A.

W Aegler of Bienne now supplied all the movements for Rolex watches. Thanks to the popularity of the wrist watch, Aegler also supplied many other companies, who accepted Aegler's guarantee that the movements were in good working order. Not so Rolex. All movements had to undergo another battery of meticulous tests over a seven-day period before Rolex would accept them. Any irregularity whatsoever and they were returned to the workshops. Once accepted, the movements were cased in traditional Swiss style and provided with crystals and bracelets. It is largely thanks to these dual methods of quality control that Rolex was able to achieve such high standards of accuracy and make such advances in horological circles. In fact, Rolex itself seemed to be setting the industry standards through its constant efforts at improving those standards.

W Rolex believed that there were three vital components to a good watch — precision, waterproofness and automatic winding. The first and arguably the most important precision had been achieved with the Class A Award but what about the other two? Wilsdorf maintained that these three factors were so interdependent that one was rendered almost useless without the other two.

W Since the invention of the first timepiece, horologists had been aware of the problems caused to the most sensitive parts, namely the crown and the winding system, by dust and damp. They had tried various methods such as fitting dust caps and making the case in one piece but to no avail. A solution eluded them.

W Wilsdorf recognised that a watch was only as good as its case for these precision movements needed maximum protection. Unlike the clock mechanism or even the pocket watch, which were by comparison well protected from the elements, needed to protect against these dangers not only to give the movement adequate protection but also to give it durability for these wrist chronometers should be as durable as their predecessors. This became even more necessary for Wilsdorf's company when his business expanded as far as Africa and the Far East. Because it took so long for the ships from England to arrive at these foreign markets, 50% of the wrist-watch cargo arrived rusted. Thus he resolved to develop a water — and weather proof wristwatch. Until the appearance of the wristwatch, in fact the solution had escaped horologists and indeed they had steered clear of the issue, having been beaten by it already once before.

W Wilsdorf personally supervised research into this perplexing problem and in 1926 history was made with the creation of the Rolex "Oyster". In this watch, the winding crown was screwed down onto the case using a twin lock system. As the name implies, the watch was totally protected from the environment since the case was air tight as well as waterproof. In developing the Rolex Oyster, Rolex also invented equipment to test the smallest fault in the case itself. Amounts of water as little as 0.05 milligrammes could be detected inside the case when the watch was immersed in water.

♛ Confidence in the name Rolex had grown considerably. In 1925, after an intensive advertising campaign, the Rolex trademark was launched and by 1927, all Rolex watches carried the name inside the case and on the movement and dial.

♛ The following year Mercedes Gleitze, a young London stenographer, wore a Rolex Oyster during her cross channel swim. This event made world headlines, for upon reaching the other side, after having been immersed in salt water for 15 hours, the watch was still keeping perfect time! Sales were better than ever. To further impress the public, Rolex Oysters were displayed in jewellers' windows inside aquariums. As the goldfish swam around, the watches were seen to be keeping perfect time. If this didn't convince the public of the watch's waterproof capabilities, nothing could. Rolex Oysters are now guaranteed to a depth of 100 metres.

♛ Although many people still regarded the waterproof watch as a bit of a joke with nothing at all to do with time keeping, Wilsdorf knew otherwise. He knew this was a revolution for the point of a waterproof watch is not so much to protect against water but against dust, sand and anything that can damage the movement. Today, almost every brand has waterproof watches on offer.

♛ The Rolex Oyster passed another feat of endurance with "flying" colours. Lieutenant Cathcart Jones wore a Rolex Oyster during his London to Melbourne return flight. After a 25,000 mile journey through all weathers, the watch was inaccurate by only a few seconds. Since then, Rolex Oysters have accompained men and women up the highest mountains and into the depths of the seas.

♛ Having solved the question of how to protect the movements of a wristwatch, Rolex set about tackling the idea of self-winding. Abram-Louis Perrelet Senior, a watch maker of Le Locle first invented a self-winding mechanism in the mid 1800s. Abram-Louis

Breguet in Paris and Recordon in London then perfected the system, which only remained fashionable for around twenty years because the mechanism was rather too delicate.

⬙ The most recent advances in self-winding had been made after the first World War by Englishman John Harwood. Wilsdorf however discarded this hammer-jerk principle as impractical. He considered for a truly self-winding watch to be completely automatic, silent, able to revolve in both directions, smooth in action and completely dispensing with buffer springs. There was also the problem of the constant movement of the wrist to be considered. The mechamism should be more robust and more practical and some method had to be found to prevent the mainspring from overwinding.

⬙ The Prince, developed in 1928, was an excellent seller with its dual dial and rectangular case. It earned for itself the title "The watch for a gentleman of distinction".

⬙ In 1931, this final obstacle was surmounted when Mr. Emile Borer, the technical head of Rolex, invented the "Rotor" whose winding mass could turn both clockwise and counter-clockwise and pivot freely on its staff in the centre of the movement. The new device was semicircular, its equilibrium unstable so that, with gravity, it would fall freely into a new position eliminating all jerking novements. The Rolex "Perpetual" had been born.

⬙ This final discovery complemented the other two since it was found that, as the tension on the mainspring was more constant than in a watch wound by hand every twenty-four hours, it was even more accurate. The owner had simply to move his or her arm to ensure the watch was wound. With the Oyster perpetual, a whole new range was developed. Today, many manufacturers incorporate the rotor principle in their self-winding watches.

Nineteen thirty-one then saw the complete justification of the wristwatch. It was been proved beyond all doubt that the wristwatch could function with chronometer accuracy, that it could be waterproof and that it could be self-winding; and perhaps even more important, that such watches could be produced on a commerical basis for sale. Since then, Rolex has created many new models incorporating innovative features. By May 1932, a Rolex watch had become the first ever to have been awarded first class certificates from the four observatories of Kew, Geneva, Neuchatel and Besancon. During the 30's, Rolex exports to the East were very successful with this market accepting eagerly every new model. Although exports to China ceased with the outbreak of the Sino-Japanese war, other Eastern countries continued to provide customers.

1944 brought personal tragedy for Wilsdorf. His wife died unexpectedly after a four-day illness, leaving him no children. But for Wilsdorf, even sorrow was an incentive to progress. Unwilling to leave Rolex to the direction of strangers after his dealth, he decided in 1945 to transfer all of his shares in the company to the newly created Hans Wilsdorf Foundation. He chose a governing council for the institution and gave precise instructions as to the distribution of funds.

The Hans Wilsdorf Foundation allocates a large sum to charities in memory of the founder's wife. Monies are also presented to horological institutions such as the Geneva School of Watchmaking, the technical section of the Geneva School of Decorative Art, The Faculty of Economic and Social Sciences of Geneva University, The Swiss Laboratory of Horological Research at Neuchatel. The Foundations generosity have provided a talking library for the blind, the preparation and realization of the complete equipment for a laboratory for the Geneva School of Watchmaking, prizes and contributions to certain Geneva professional schools and gifts of cinematographic and radio apparatus to charities.

Wilsdorf's charitable endeauors,

though admirable, were still only a sideline to his neverending desire to prefect his watches. The Rolex Datejust, in 1945, was the first wristwatch to display the date on its dial. The Rolex Datejust, waterproof and self-winding, shows the date which automatically changes at midnight.

Although exports declined during World War II, Rolex recovered, expanding business to Tokyo and the Far East on a large scale. The company produces many unusual case designs, but emphasized day, date, month, moonphase watches in oyster and precision cases. The 50's saw the advance development of the oyster perpetual with date in a smaller and somewhat flatter case. This basic model held the future success of the company and it made several variations in steel, steel & gold and gold with different bracelets. In 1952, the Rolex Turnagraph, later called the Submarine 100, was developed. Guaranteed to a depth of 330 feet, it was used by skindivers. A ladies' perpetual oyster, with the same variations as the men's, was introduced in 1954 and the GMT-Master, for pilots, in 1955.

1956 saw the introduction of the first day — date chronometer to have the day written on the dial in full as well as the president bracelet, of the kind presented to President Dwight D. Eisenhower to celebrate his reelection.

In 1959, the Submariner case was improved with the Rolex crown guard which protected the screw-down, twinlock winding crown from damage during under-water exploration. On January 23rd 1960, Professor Piccard's bathscaph Trieste dove to a depth of 35,800 feet in the Pacific Oceans Marianas Trench. A special Rolex Oyster was attached to the Trieste during the record-breaking dive. The watch emerged unharmed and keeping perfect time having resisted a pressure greater than seven tons per square inch.

With the experience of 84 years, Rolex has earned more certificates for observatory-quality chronometers than all other companies combined. The quality and value of a Rolex and the status of owning one have made Rolex the most renowned wristwatch manufacturer in the world. The name Rolex is registered in Bienne and the crown is registered in Geneve; the two are combined in today's Rolex.

In this modern age when many things are produced as quickly as possible, Rolex still prides itself on the fact that it takes a year to finish each chronometer wristwatch because they are checked and rechecked to assure that they are the world's most accurate. This attention to perfection is due to the determination of Hans Wilsdorf who believed that quality and pride in manufacturing was essential to produce Rolex wristwatches. To date, the company has manufactured over six-million certified chronometers and well over twelve million wristwatches in total.

ROLL OF HONOUR

Autumn 1905	**LONDON** Nation-wide launching of the Rolex wristlet watch on the British market.
Spring 1907	**LA CHAUX DE FONDS** Hans Wilsdorf opens his Swiss office
Winter 1908	**LONDON** Wilsdorf coins the word "Rolex"
March 22, 1910	**OFFICIAL CONTROLMENT OFFICE FOR THE RATING OF WATCHES, BIENNE** The 1st Rolex wrist-watch chronometer to be officially controlled obtains a 1st Class Certificate (11" round)
July 15, 1914	**KEW OBSERVATORY** Rolex obtains the first Class "A" Observatory Certificate ever awarded for a wristwatch chronometer (11" round), after testing for 45 days in 5 timing positions and 3 temperatures. This test is identical to that applied to large marine chronometers, no allowance being made for wrist-watch movements.
Summer 1919	**GENEVA** Rolex moves to 18 rue de Marche
May 2, 1925	**GENEVA** Rolex trademark the crown is launched
June 14, 1925	**KEW OBSERVATORY** Rolex obtains the first Class "A" Observatory Certificate ever awarded for so small a chronometer (5-3/4" oval). The annual report of the Kew Observatory that year mentioned this feat in the following terms: "It is interesting to note that a Class 'A' Certificate has been awarded to Rolex for a small oval movement measuring 5-3/4". This is the smallest movement which has obtained a Class 'A' Certificate at the Observatory in the last few years." By 1925, Rolex had therefore already proved that a small ladies' watch can be endowed with the properties of an extremely fine chronometer.
July 29, 1926	**SWITZERLAND** Rolex registers the Oyster and is issued a patent for the world's first waterproof case
March 16, 1927	**KEW OBSERVATORY** The first Class "A" Observatory Certificate ever awarded with the mention "specially good" for a 6-3/4" wrist-watch chronometer. This result was commented on as follows in the annual Kew report: "Another remarkable

result recorded this year was the awarding of a Class 'A' Certificate with mention 'specially good' to a 6-3/4'' rectangular movement submitted by Rolex, which obtained a total of 86.5 points.''

March 17, 1927 KEW OBSERVATORY
First "A" Certificate for a Rolex 10½'' (round) chronometer.

November 23, 1927 LONDON
Mercedes Gleitze swims the English channel wearing a Rolex Oyster

May 31, 1928 GENEVA OBSERVATORY
First 1st Class Certificate for a 6-3/4'' Rolex chronometer. Result obtained in the marine chronometer category (old ruling).

May 31, 1928 KEW OBSERVATORY
First "A" Certificate for a 8-3/4'' Rolex chronometer (round).

Winter 1928 SWITZERLAND
Rolex Prince with TS300 movement, ref. 971

March 11, 1929 NEUCHATEL OBSERVATORY
First 1st Class Certificate for a 6-3/4'' Rolex chronometer.

May 18, 1929 SWITZERLAND
First Rolex 9-3/4'' chronograph

Summer 1931 SWITZERLAND
Rolex Oyster Perpetual, ref. 1858, first automatic & waterproof wristwatch

May 31, 1932 BESANCON OBSERVATORY
First 1st Class Certificate for a Rolex 6-3/4'' chronometer. Rolex is the only watch to have obtained a 1st Class Certificate from the four Observatories of Kew, Geneva, Neuchatel and Besancon for a small wristlet watch.

June 23, 1934 KEW OBSERVATORY
First "A" Certificate for a 16½'', ultraflat (2.8mm.) Rolex chronometer.

February 20, 1935 NEUCHATEL OBSERVATORY
1st Class Certificate for a 16½'', ultraflat (2.8mm.) Rolex chronometer.

April 29, 1936 OFFICIAL CONTROLMENT OFFICE FOR THE RATING OF WATCHES, BIENNE
500 Rolex chronometers numbered 501-1000 ("Prince" calibre) ALL obtain

a Rating Certificate with mention "specially good". (These watches were specially manufactured for the occasion of King George V's Silver Jubilee.) Rolex thus proves that the serial manufacture of wrist-watch chronometers is possible, even within a short, given period (146 days).

December 15, 1936   KEW OBSERVATORY
"A" Certificate for T. S. chronometer, "Prince" calibre, with mention "specially good": 87.6 points. This remained record for wrist-watch chronometers of any size until 1939.

Summer 1938   SWITZERLAND
Rolex Hooded Bubbleback, ref. 3065

August 31, 1942   NEUCHATEL OBSERVATORY
1st Class Certificate for a round, 12½" chronometer: 9.65 points. The best result ever recorded for a wrist-watch chronometer of less than 13". This record was held in 1942, 1943 and 1944.

November 2, 1944   SWITZERLAND
Square chronograph, ref. 3529

January 5, 1945   OFFICIAL CONTROLMENT OFFICE FOR THE RATING OF WATCHES, BIENNE
Rolex obtains its 50,000th Rating Certificate for wrist-watch chronometers, an event unique in the history of watchmaking.

Spring 1945   SWITZERLAND
The Rolex Date just, the first waterproof, self-winding calendar wrist chronometer which charges the date in its dial window automatically.

1945   NEUCHATEL OBSERVATORY
A rectangular Rolex movement (22mm. × 38mm.) obtained the remarkable record of 8.4 points and showed the smallest variation in the position tests ever registered for a wrist-watch chronometer (0.32 seconds daily). The annual Neuchatel Observatory report for 1944 (published in the summer of 1945) mentions this result in the following terms: "We congratulate Messrs. Rolex who have specialized in the manufacture of good wristlet watches."

1947   SWITZERLAND
Rolex Oyster Moonphase, ref. 6062

1949   Rolex Day/Date/Month chronograph, precision case, ref. 4768

1949   Rolex Oyster chronograph, Day/Date/Month, ref. 4767

1950	Rolex Day/Date/Month/Moonphase chronograph, ref. 81806
1952	**SWITZERLAND** The Turnagraph later renamed Submariner 100 is made for use by scubadivers to a depth of 100m
1953	**NEPAL** New Zealander Hillary and Sherpa Tonsing, members of the British Himalayas expedition led by Sir John Hunt, were the first to reach the summit of Mt. Everest equipped with Rolex Oyster Perpetuals which functioned perfectly throughout, despite extremes of temperature and rough treatment
1954	**SWITZERLAND** The first Rolex Oyster Perpetual for ladies. The "GMT-Master" is the first calender chronometer designed specifically for pilots allowing simultaneous reading of the exact time in different zones.
1956	Rolex Oyster Perpetual Day-Date, a self winding wrist chronometer which is the first to indicate the day of the week written in full.
1960	A special Rolex Oyster fixed to the outside of the bathyscaph Trieste withstands a pressure of nearly 7 tons/sq. inch at a depth of 35,798 ft. Upon surfacing, Jacques Piccard finds the Rolex to be functioning perfectly.
1971	**SWITZERLAND** Rolex Sea Dweller, guarenteed waterproof to a depth of 2,000 ft. A patent is granted for the first diver's watch to incorporate a gas escape value used in saturation diving.
1978	Rolex Oyster quartz, guarenteed waterproof to 165 ft. The calendar analogue timepiece combines an eleven-jewelled movement and a quartz-linked motor. It operates normally in magnetic fiels up to 1000 Oersted.
1989	The number of Official Swiss Chronometer titles obtained by Rolex up to the present time represents more than half the entire production of Swiss chronometers to have been officially certified by the Swiss Institutes for Chronometer tests.

TIMELESS ELEGANCE

COLLECTION OF
ROLEX ADVERTISEMENTS

Rolex introduces for the first time the greatest Triumph in Watch-making

ROLEX 'OYSTER'

The Wonder Watch that Defies the Elements.

**MOISTURE PROOF
WATER PROOF
HEAT PROOF
VIBRATION PROOF
COLD PROOF
DUST PROOF**

*Copyright by
Pacific and
Atlantic
Photos, Ltd.*

Miss Mercedes Gleitze carried an 'Oyster' throughout her recent Channel Swim. More than ten hours of submersion under the most trying conditions failed to harm its perfect timekeeping. No moisture had penetrated and not the slightest corrosion or condensation was revealed in the subsequent examination of the Watch.

BEING hermetically sealed the Rolex 'Oyster' is proof against changes of climate, dust, water, damp, heat, moisture, cold, sand or grease; it can, in consequence, be worn in the sea or bath without injury, nor would arctic or tropical conditions affect the wonderful precision of its beautifully poised movement. The introduction of the Rolex 'Oyster' model marks an unique development in the forward stride of the chronometric science, and perfect timekeeping under all conditions is at last a possibility.

A HANDSOMELY printed, fully informative Brochure illustrating the entire range of OYSTER Models available, together with the name of nearest jeweller stocking ROLEX Watches, sent post free to any reader who makes application by postcard or letter, giving name and address to our London Office:

THE ROLEX WATCH CO. Ltd.

**40/44,
Holborn Viaduct,
London, E.C.4.**

For MEN or WOMEN.

Send for this coloured Brochure it's FREE!

THE ROLEX OYSTER

ROLEX OYSTER PRICES

The Silver:
£5.15.0
9-ct. Gold:
£10.10.0
18-ct. Gold:
£15.15.0

Fitted with good quality strong leather straps for Men, or Moire Silk bands for Women. If fitted with the fashionable new "FRAYPRUF" (regd.) Woven Flexible Wire Milanese Gold-Filled Bands (White or Yellow) 20/- extra to above.

THE ROLEX WATCH CO. LTD. LONDON, ENGLAND

The Practical
WATCH & CLOCK MAKER

No. 7   SEPTEMBER 15th, 1928   Vol. I.

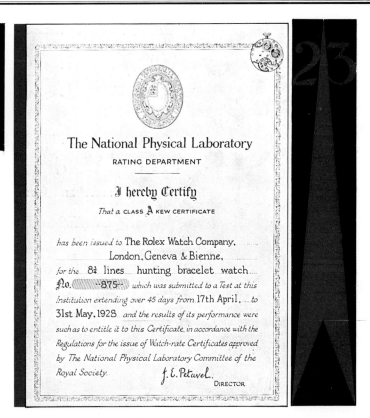
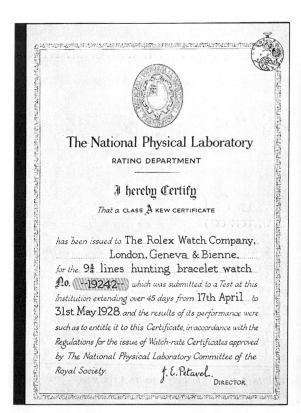

The Practical
WATCH & CLOCK MAKER

| No. 20 | OCTOBER 15th, 1929 | Vol. II. |

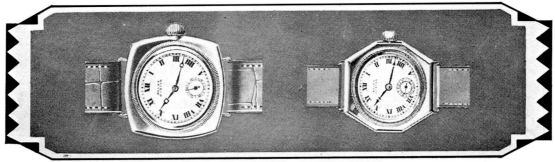

The Practical
WATCH & CLOCK MAKER

| No. 28 | JUNE 15th, 1930 | Vol. III. |

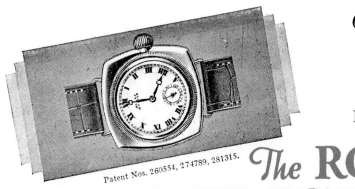

Choose the best by *every* test –

ROLEX

PRECISION WRISTLETS

REG'D TRADE MARK

25 WORLD'S RECORDS FOR ACCURACY

No. 5. Curved to wrist.
Silver . . . £4 15 0
9 ct. . . . £9 15 0
18 ct. . . £13 15 0

No. 9.
Silver . . . £4 10 0
9 ct. . . . £8 10 0
18 ct. . . . £12 0 0

No. 77.
9 ct. . . . £8 15 0
18 ct. . . . £12 10 0

THE ROLEX 'OYSTER'

WATERPROOF — DUSTPROOF
Patent Nos. 260554, 274789–281315.
Snowite, £5 15 0
9 ct., £10 10 0   18 ct., £15 15 0
SIZES FOR MEN AND WOMEN

No. 7.
Silver . . . £3 10 0
9 ct. . . . £7 10 0
18 ct. . . . £11 0 0

No. 6.
9 ct. . . . £8 8 0
18 ct. . . . £10 10 0

No. 33.
9 ct. . . . £6 6 0
18 ct. . . . £8 8 0

No. 80.
9 ct. . . . £7 7 0

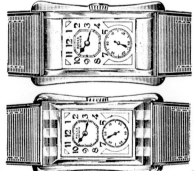

No. 83.
9 ct. . . . £7 7 0

No. 90.
9 ct. . . . £9 9 0
18 ct. . . . £11 11 0

THE ROLEX 'PRINCE'

The only wrist-watch known to horological science as 'Observatory Grade'—a superfine production and a worthy gift in recognition of exceptional service. The ideal wrist-watch for the Medical Profession.

Solid Platinum £65 0 0
18 ct. White & Yellow Gold . £21 0 0
9 ct. Gold £14 14 0
Untarnishable Sterling Silver £8 8 0
Swiss Government Observation Certificate with every 'Prince.'

No. 86.
9 ct. . . . £8 8 0
18 ct. . . . £10 10 0

No. 91.
9 ct. . . . £9 9 0
18 ct. . . . £11 11 0

No. 67.
9 ct. . . . £10 10 0
18 ct. . . . £12 12 0

STOCKED BY ALL GOOD JEWELLERS & AT THE SAME PRICES THROUGHOUT THE BRITISH EMPIRE

Sole Agents for India: J. Boseck & Co., Calcutta; Lund & Blockley, Bombay; P. Orr & Sons, Ltd., Madras and Rangoon.

See name ROLEX on dial and movement. If any difficulty in obtaining write to The Rolex Watch Co., Ltd., 40-44, Holborn Viaduct, London, E.C.1, FOR NAME OF NEAREST AGENT.
Insist on the genuine Rolex—Refuse Substitutes.

THE ROLEX WATCH CO., LTD. (H. WILSDORF, Managing Director) GENEVA & LONDON

The Practical
WATCH & CLOCK MAKER

| No. 15 | MAY 15th, 1929 | Vol. II. |

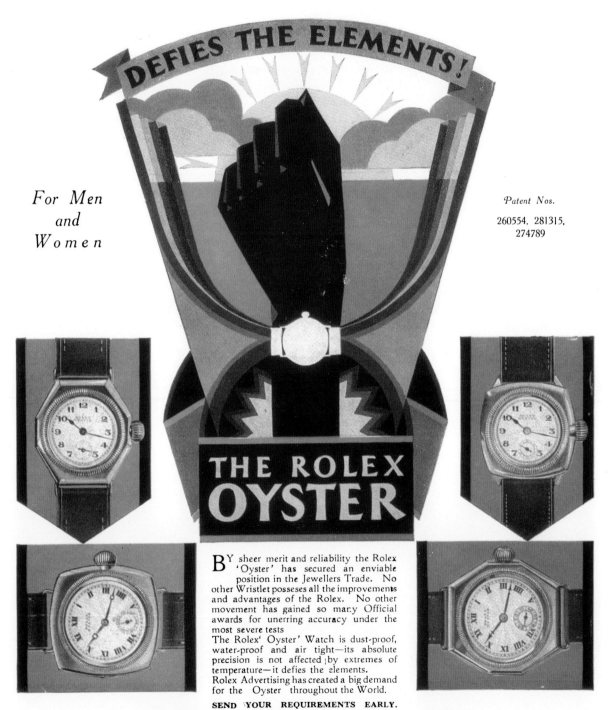

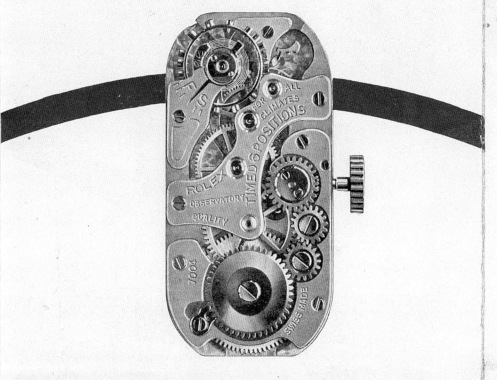

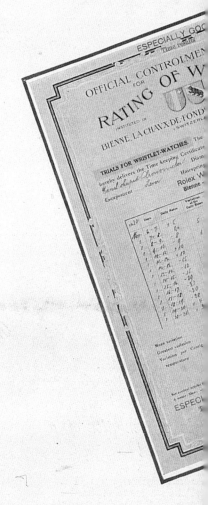

POINTS *of* INTEREST

1   Quite different in shape from any other movement. The second hand moves within the periphery of a separate dial, so that hour and minute hands cannot interfere with or cover the second hand.

2   Plenty of room for large wheels, and no overcrowding in the disposition of the many component parts. The movement fills the inner case up completely so that no empty space is left for harbouring dust and other impurities.

3   A very large chronometer balance-wheel, quite as big as usually fitted to pocket chronometers, gives perfect compensation and vacillation and ensures precision time. It is provided with 16 very heavy screws.

4   The hairspring is made of that " Elinvar " metal, invented by the world-famous Professeur Guillaume, which is almost completely unaffected by temperatures and other influences.

5   The escapement—the heart of a watch—is a true masterpiece of horological science.

6   The jewels are prima quality red rubies, especially well polished by hand, each one adjusted to its respective pivot by Rolex precision instruments, measured by the thousandth part of a millimetre.

7   Every Rolex Prince movement is submitted to a Swiss Government Observation Station for test, and only when a certificate of Super-Excellence is issued by these independent scientists is it ready for sale.

ALEX

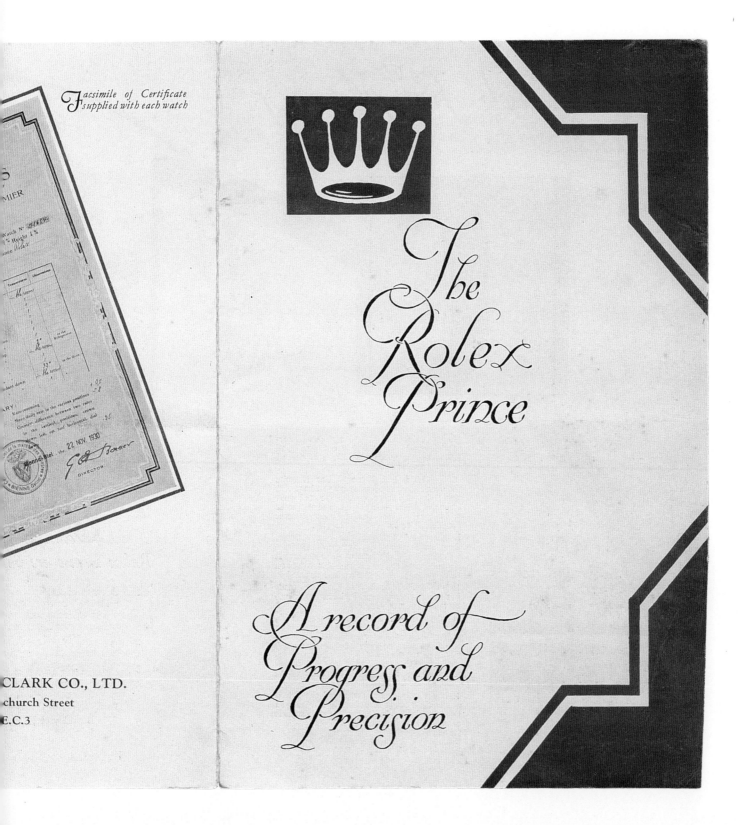

MIER

Watch N°

Height

22 NOV. 1930

DIRECTOR

CLARK CO., LTD.

church Street

E.C.3

The
Rolex
Prince

A record of
Progress and
Precision

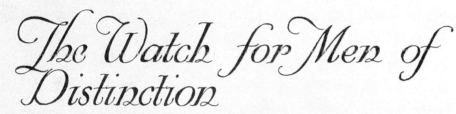

The Watch for Men of Distinction

"A"

"A"

18-*ct. Gold*	£25 0 0
9-*ct. Gold*	17 Gns.
Silver	10 Gns.

A Swiss Government Certificate with each Watch

 IKE a real Prince, this super-grade Rolex stands out among all other watches for sheer merit and distinction.

Its beautiful curved line is quite different from any other watch you have ever seen; it just fits caressingly around your wrist and makes you feel as if you hated to be without it after having once become accustomed to its comfortable grip.

It goes for 58 hours with one winding, therefore twice as long as any other wrist-watch, and if you forget to wind it there is no need to worry, as the Prince will tick on merrily and precisely for another day.

It is the only wristwatch in the world made in the most superfine quality known to science as " Observatory Grade."

It is set in 15 real red fine quality rubies, and provided with a heavy chronometer balance with 16 heavy screws for compensation. Its hairspring is made of that famous " Elinvar " metal which was invented by Professeur Guillaume of Paris, and gained for him the elevation to the rank of an Officer of the Legion d'Honneur.

It is perfectly compensated, and the Prince will be right to the very second, whether you live in sweltering India, in the Arctic regions or in foggy London.

Occasions f

Rolex Prince are pa

1. A token of appreciation
" Prince " being provide
a particular favourite wit
will give equal pleasure

2. As a gift to your son w
you are particularly pro

3. To your son-in-law as a

4. A gift to men in recogni
in very many instances,
with dignity.

5. As a Birthday or Xmas

It's Perfect Accuracy

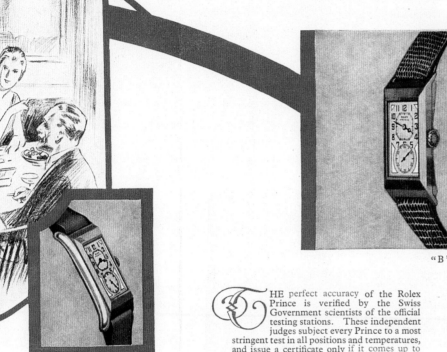

"B"

the Presentation of a

favoured —

or after a serious illness. The
Pulse-reading second hand is
profession. No other present
circumstances.

achieved something of which

ces of particular merit, which,
s to know how to recompense

THE perfect accuracy of the Rolex
Prince is verified by the Swiss
Government scientists of the official
testing stations. These independent
judges subject every Prince to a most
stringent test in all positions and temperatures,
and issue a certificate only if it comes up to
their very rigorous Observatory standard.

During 1930 no less than 3,574 Rolex WRIST
Watches obtained Official Swiss Government
Timing Certificates, and of that number
41½ per cent. secured the further distinction of
" especially good "—a rare and remarkable
achievement.

The Prince is therefore a real Prince amongst
all watches by sheer merit and distinction, and
not simply because its manufacturers choose
to imagine it to be so.

It has two separate dials : one for the hour and
minute hands, and one for the second hand, so
that the Prince will enable you to test to the
fractions of seconds any sporting events, to
make scientific observations, or to allow your
doctor to register the beat of your pulse or
heart. There is no other watch but the Prince,
which by its ingenious and patented construc-
tion, will enable you to do these things ; now
no longer are any special instruments necessary.

"B"

18-ct. Gold	£22 15 0
9-ct. Gold	15 Gns.
Silver	10 Gns.

*A spare Strap and Glass supplied
with each Watch*

CERTIFICATES

OFFICIAL CONTROLMENT OFFICES
FOR
THE
RATING OF WATCHES

INSTITUTED IN   THE TOWNS OF

BIENNE, LA CHAVX-DE-FONDS, LE LOCLE, ST. IMIER
(SWITZERLAND)

FIRST CLASS TRIALS.   The Office of _Bienne-Biel_

hereby delivers the Time keeping Certificate N° _2701_ for the Movement N° _100089_

„_Prince Imperial_"   Diameter of Movement _37,3_ ᵐ/ₘ Height _4,8_ ᵐ/ₘ

Escapement _Lever_   Hairspring _Breguet Bolinvar_   Balance _Rolex_

Rolex Watch Co. Ltd.

Bienne - Geneva - London - Paris

19 33	Days	Daily Rates	Variations of the Daily Rates	Positions			Temperatures	Observations
July	12—13	+ 3,7		Vertical, Pendant up			in the room	
1	13—14	+ 1,4	2,3	"	"	"	/	
1	14—15	− 0,3	1,7	"	"	"	/	
1	15—16	+ 0,8	1,1	"	"	"	/	
1	16—17	− 5,5		"	"	left	/	
1	17—18	− 5		"	"	right	/	
1	18—19	0,0		Horizontal, Dial down			/	
1	19—20	+ 7,5		"	"	up	/	
1	20—21	+ 7	0,5	"	"	"	/	
1	21—22	+ 6,7	0,3	"	"	"	/	
1	22—23	+ 6,3		"	"	"	2°	in the Refrigerator
1	23—24	+ 6		"	"	"	in the room	
1	24—25	+ 6,4		"	"	"	32°	in the Oven
1	25—26	− 0,4		Vertical, Pendant up			in the room	
1	26—27	− 1		"	"	"		

SUMMARY :

Mean daily rate in the positions pendant up and dial up . . . . . .   + 3,8

Mean variation of the daily rates . . . .   ± 1,18

Greatest variation   2,3

Difference between the mean rates in the horizontal positions . . . . . .   − 7,1

Difference between the mean rates in the vertical positions, pendant up and pendant left . . . .   − 6,9

Difference between the mean rates in vertical positions, pendant up and pendant right . . . .   − 6,4

Difference between flat and hanging positions . . . .   − 7

Variation per Centigrade degree of temperature   0,00

Secondary error . . . .   + 0,8

Rate-resuming . . . .   − 2,4

See overleaf the Abstracts from the Regulations.

+ means: Fast; — means: Slow.

Bienne-Biel,

The Observatory Timekeeping stated on this Official Certificate has been reexamined and found correct.   **Rolex Watch Co. Ltd.** Geneva-Switzerland.

Dated NOV 193_

G. A. Borner

DIRECTOR.

Abstracts from the Regulations referring to the Deposit and Examination of the Rating of Watches.

Art. 1. — The Official Controlment Offices, instituted in the towns of Bienne, La Chaux-de-Fonds, Le Locle and St-Imier receive, on deposit, the watches sent to them for the purpose of submitting these watches to various trials in order to control their running and to ascertain their time-keeping qualities.

The aforesaid Offices may also accept for control other time measuring apparatus. Should the mode of observing be different from that prescribed by the Regulations, the Offices will only deliver returns on their note paper, with printed heading.

Art. 5. — The rating of each watch is compared every 24 hours with the indications of a main-clock checked daily according to a signal from the Neuchâtel Astronomical and Chronometric Observatory.

Details of Trials and their Duration (Art. 8 & 12).

				1st Class Trials	Trials for 8 days' Watches	
Vertical	position, Pendant up, Ambient temperature (in the room)			4 days	7 days	wound up on first day
»	»	» left, »	» » » »	1 »	1 »	wound up
»	»	» right, [»	» » » »	1 »	1 »	» »
Horizontal	»	Dial down, »	» » » »	1 »	1 »	
»	»	Dial up, »	» » » »	3 »	7 »	wound up on first day
»	»	» » In Refrigerator, temperature from + 1º to + 4º C (+ 34º to + 39º Fahr)		1 »	1 »	wound up
»	»	» » Ambient » (in the room)		1 »	1 »	» »
»	»	» » In Oven, » from + 28º to + 32º C (+ 82º to + 89º Fahr)		1 »	1 »	» »
Vertical	»	Pendant up, Ambient » (in the room)		1 »	1 »	
»	»	» » » » » » »		1 »	2 »	wound up
			Duration of Trials	15 days	22 days	

Details of Trials and their Duration for Wristlet or Bracelet Watches (Art. 13).

Vertical	position	» Crown down, Ambient temperature (in the room)		2 days
»	»	» left, » » »		2 »
»	»	» up, » » » »		2 »
Horizontal	»	Dial down, » » » »		2 »
»	»	» up, » » » »		2 »
»	»	» » In Refrigerator, temperature from + 1º to + 4º Centigrade (+ 34º to + 39º Fahr.)		1 »
»	»	» » Ambient temperature (in the room)		1 »
»	»	» » In oven, temperature from + 28º to + 32º Centigrade (+ 82º to + 89º Fahr.)		1 »
Vertical	»	Crown down, Ambient temperature (in the room)		2 »
			Duration of Trials	15 days

Limits for obtaining a Certificate (Art. 8, 9, 12 & 13).

	1st Class	1st Class complicated movts. and movts. of special sizes	8 Days' Watches	Wristlet Watches
Mean Daily rate, in the vertical pendant up and horizontal dial up positions, ambient temperature of the room before the thermical tests.	— 4 sec. to + 10 sec.	— 5 sec. to + 12 sec.	— 5 sec. to + 10 sec.	—
Mean variation	3	4	7	15 sec.
Greatest variation	5	6	10	20
Difference between mean rates, horizontal positions, dial up and dial down	10	13	10	30
Difference between mean rates in vertical position pendant up and vertical positions, pendant left and pendant right	20	25	25	—
Difference between flat and vertical positions	10	13	10	
Variation per Centigrade degree of temperature	0,5	0,7	0,5	1,5
Secondary error	9	11	9	—
Rate-Resuming	5	8	10	20
Mean daily rate in the various positions and in the ambient temperature of the room				— 10 to + 30
Greatest difference between two rates in the vertical positions, pendant down, pendant left, pendant up and horizontal dial down				50

Art. 9. — **Complicated watches and Movements of special sizes.**

a) complicated watches;

b) watches with movements the height of which does not exceed 4,3 millimeters, measured from the lower portion of the plate to the highest piece;

c) watches of small sizes, the largest casing dimension of which does not exceed 30 millimeters, are accepted for 1st. class trials within the above limits (see 1st. class limits for complicated movements and movements of special sizes).

Art. 10. — Chronographs and other watches certain functions of which may be interrupted, are observed during the last day of the trials, in the vertical position, pendant up, before the thermical tests with all the mechanisms running. The daily rate and the corresponding variation of that day are taken into account when recording results.

Art. 14. — Watches the rates of which keep within one half of the limits required to obtain a Certificate, are awarded the additional distinction: « **Especially good running results** ».

Adopted at a meeting of the General Council of St-Imier, October 17th 1932.

FOR AND IN BEHALF OF THE GENERAL COUNCIL:

N. Frepp, *For the Secretary.*   **E. Chapuis,** *President.*

Adopted by the General Council of La Chaux-de-Fonds, at their meeting of December 1st 1932.

FOR AND IN BEHALF OF THE GENERAL COUNCIL:

A. Naine, *Secretary.*   **L. Morf,** *President.*

Adopted by the General Council of Le Locle, at their meeting of October 21st 1932.

FOR AND IN BEHALF OF THE GENERAL COUNCIL:

A. Marguier, *Secretary.*   **M. Inäbnit,** *President.*

APPROVED THE ABOVE.

Berne, October 18th 1932.

FOR AND IN BEHALF OF THE EXECUTIVE COUNCIL:

Hans Steiner, *Secretary.*   **Dr H. Mouttet,** *President.*

SANCTIONED THIS DAY,

Neuchâtel, December 16th 1932.

FOR AND IN BEHALF OF THE STATE COUNCIL:

Studer-Jeanrenaud, *Secretary.*   **A. Clottu,** *President.*

Any persons infringing the copyright of this certificate will be proceeded against, according to civil and penal law.

OFFICIAL CONTROLMENT OFFICES
FOR
THE
RATING OF WATCHES

INSTITUTED IN.   THE TOWNS OF

BIENNE, LA CHAVX-DE-FONDS, LE LOCLE, ST. IMIER
(SWITZERLAND)

TRIALS FOR WRISTLET-WATCHES. The Office of _Bienne-Biel_

hereby delivers the Time keeping Certificate N° _18683_ for the Watch N° _1639_

„Rolex Prince"   Diameter of Movement _16,9-32,7_ ‰ Height _4,2_ ‰

Escapement _Lever_   Hairspring _Autocompensating_ Balance _Rolex_

Rolex Watch Co. Ltd.

Bienne - Geneva - London - Paris

19 _38_ Days	Daily Rates	Variations of the Daily Rates	Positions			Temperatures	Observations
July 29 – 30	– 9		Vertical, Crown down			_in the room_	
„ 30 – 31	– 12	3	„ „ „			„	
„ 31 – 1	+ 3		„ „ left			„	
August 1 – 2	+ 1	2	„ „ „			„	
„ 2 – 3	– 6		„ „ up			„	
„ 3 – 4	– 6	0	„ „ „			„	
„ 4 – 5	– 6		Horizontal, Dial down			„	
„ 5 – 6	– 6	0	„ „ „			„	
„ 6 – 7	+ 6		„ „ up			„	
„ 7 – 8	– 2	8	„ „ „			„	
„ 8 – 9	– 1		„ „ „			_2°_	in the Refrigerator
„ 9 – 10	– 3		„ „ „			_in the room_	
„ 10 – 11	0		„ „ „			_32°_	in the Oven
„ 11 – 12	– 12		Vertical, Crown down			_in the room_	
„ 12 – 13	– 11		„ „ „			„	

SUMMARY :

Mean daily rate in the different positions . . . . _-3,7_

Mean variation . . . . _± 2,60_

Greatest variation . . . . _8_

Difference between the mean rates in the horizontal positions, dial up and dial down . . . . . . _-8_

Greatest difference between two rates in the vertical positions, crown down, left, up, and horizontal dial down . . . . _15_

Variation per Centigrade degree of temperature . . . . _+0,03_

Rate-resuming . . . . _-0,5_

See overleaf the Abstracts from the Regulations.
+ means : Fast ; — means ; Slow.

ESPECIALLY GOOD
Time results

Bienne-Biel, the _15 AOÛT 1938_ 19

G. A. Berner

DIRECTOR.

JUBILEE COLLECTION

The Jubilee Section of this book
was copied from a Rolex catalog published
in 1946

The photographs illustration of the Jubilee Section were taken by A. Grivel, Geneva.

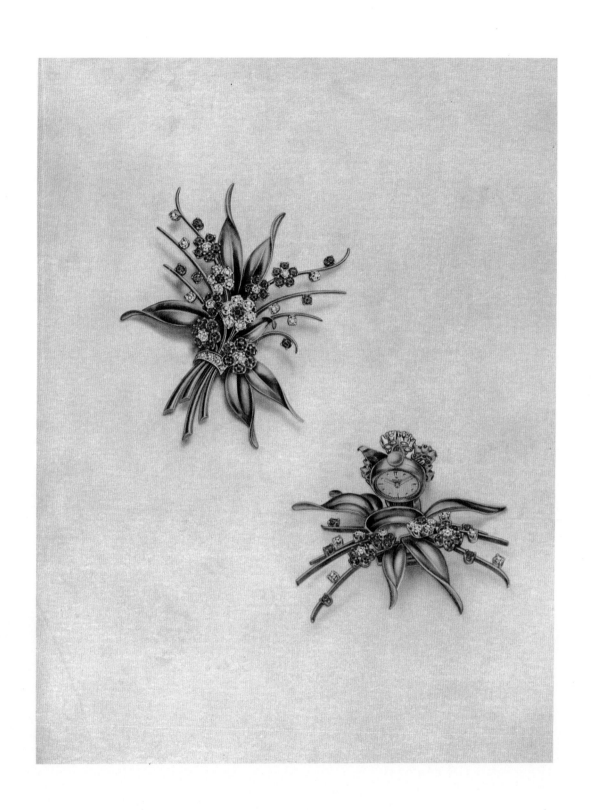

PLATE 1

Ref. 4281   (Registered model)

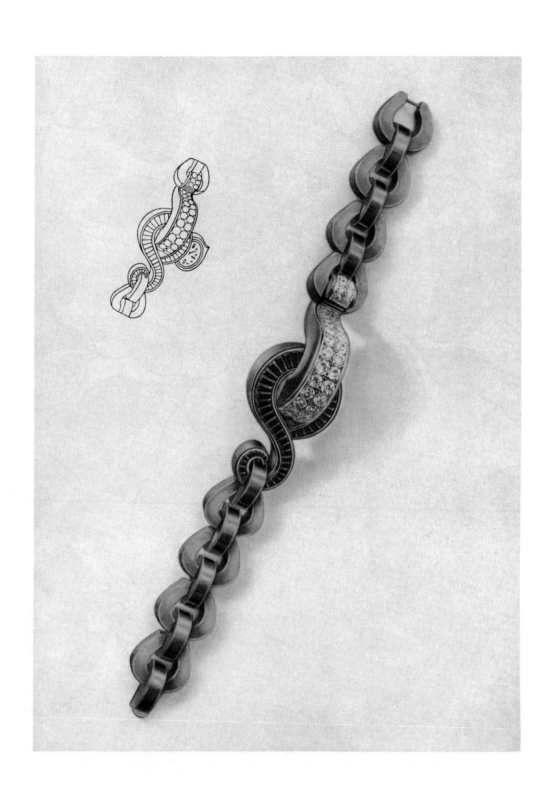

PLATE 2

Ref. 4407   (Registered model)

PLATE 3

Ref. 4394   (Registered model)

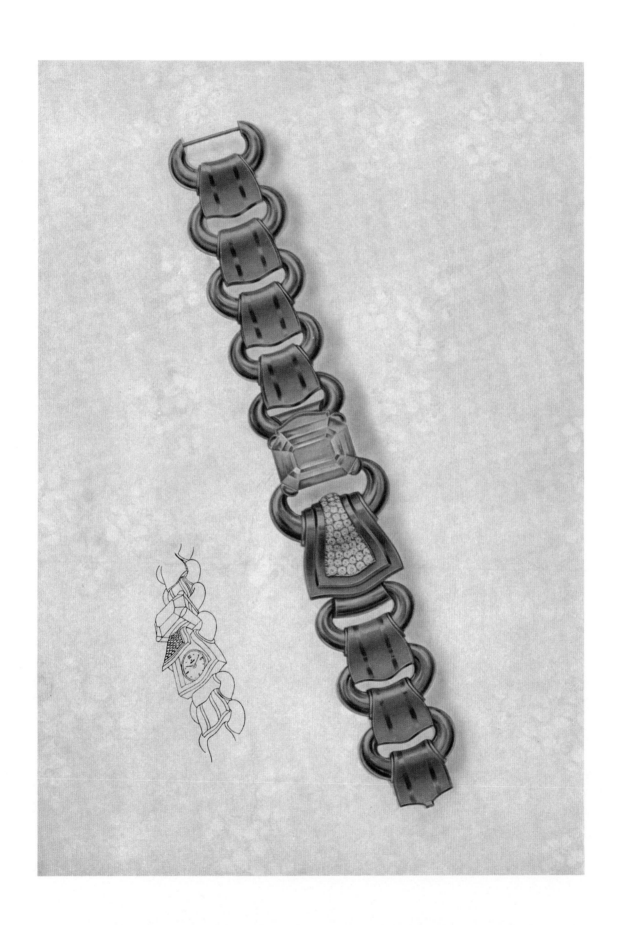

PLATE 4

Ref. 4336   (Registered model)

PLATE 5

Ref. 3771 (Registered model)

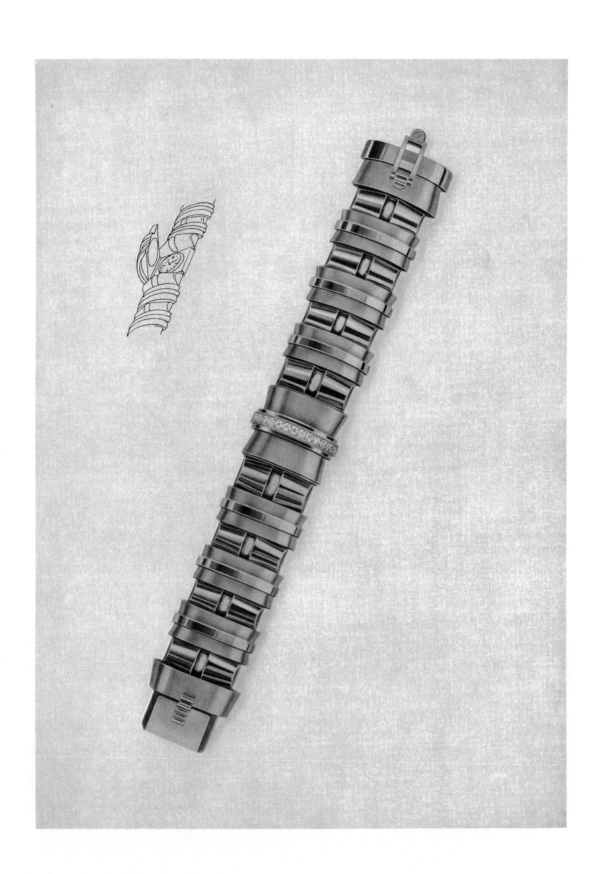

PLATE 6

Ref. 4484   (Registered model)

PLATE 7

Ref. 4473   (Registered model)

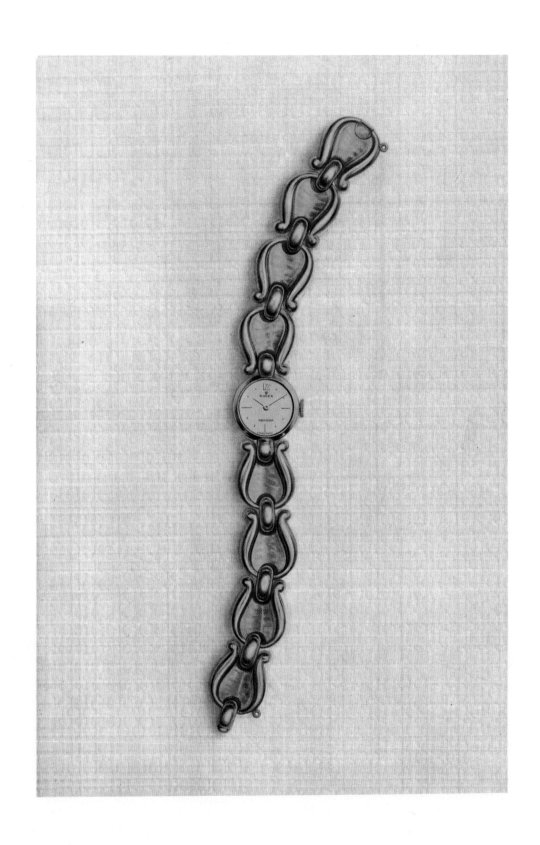

PLATE 8

Ref. 4374   (Registered model)

PLATE 9
Ref. 4491 (Registered model)   Ref. 4495 (Registered model)

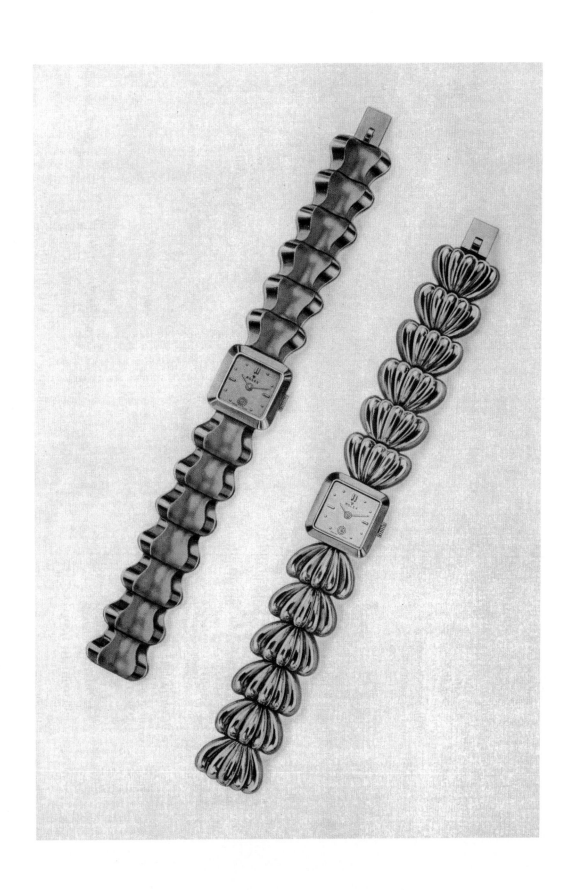

PLATE 10

Ref. 4496 (Registered model)   Ref. 4493 (Registered model)

73

PLATE 11

Ref. 4492 (Registered model)   Ref. 4494 (Registered model)

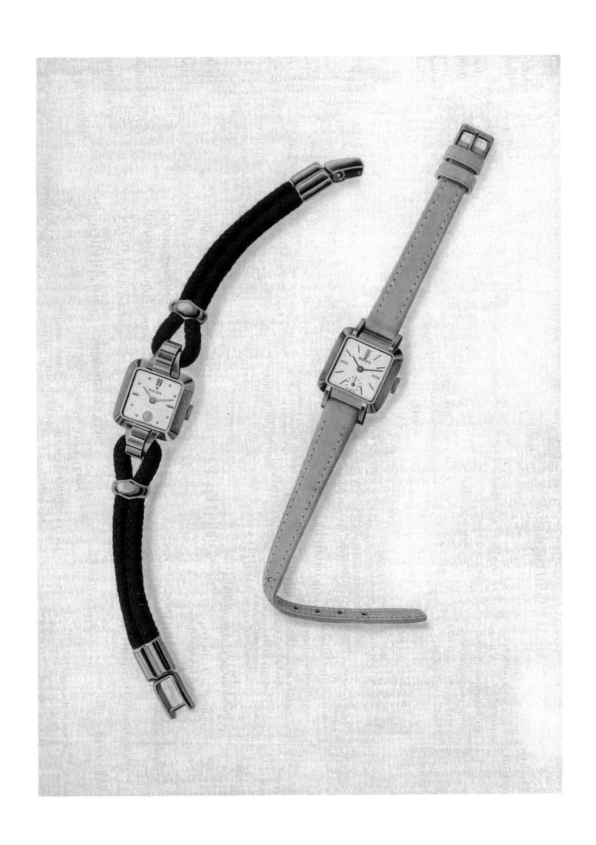

PLATE 12

Ref. 4381   Ref. 4391

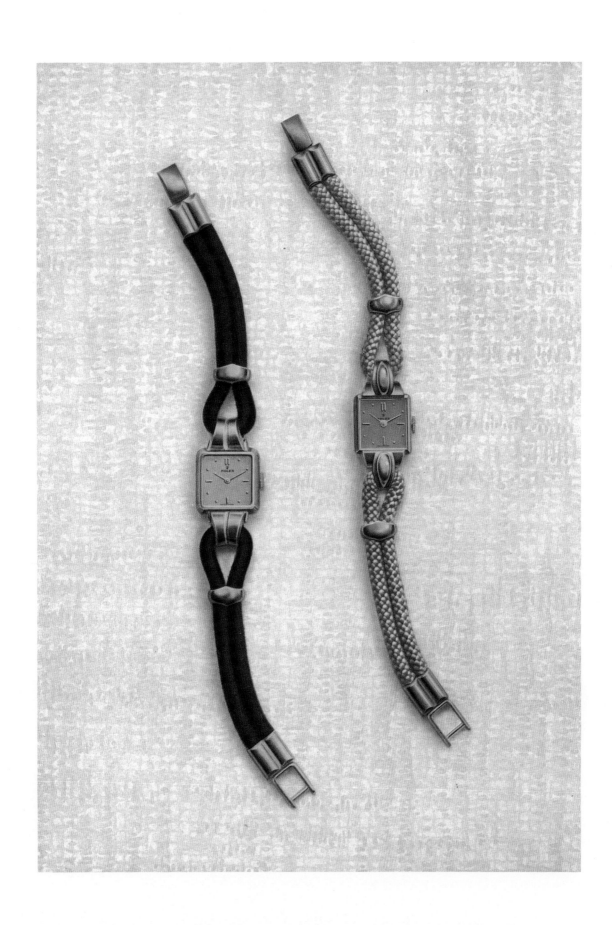

PLATE 13

Ref. 4405   Ref. 4211 (Registered model)

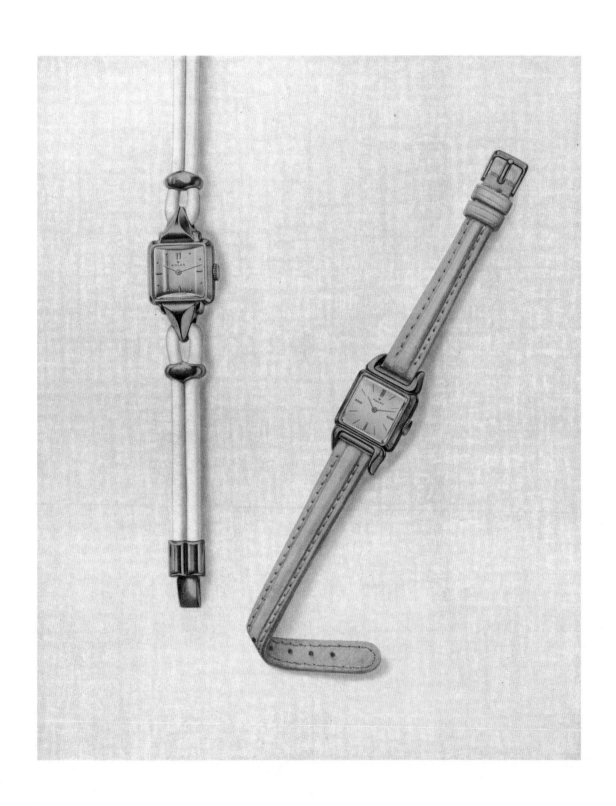

PLATE 14

Ref. 4454 (Registered model)   Ref. 4401

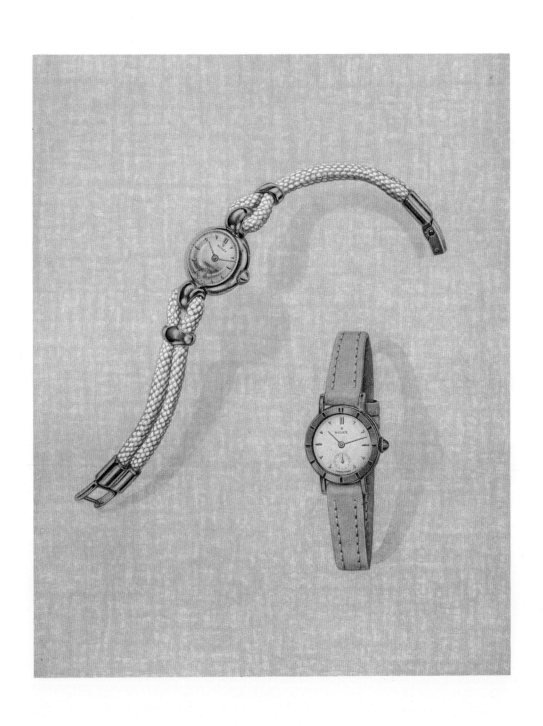

PLATE 15

Ref. 4323   Ref. 4327 (Registered model)

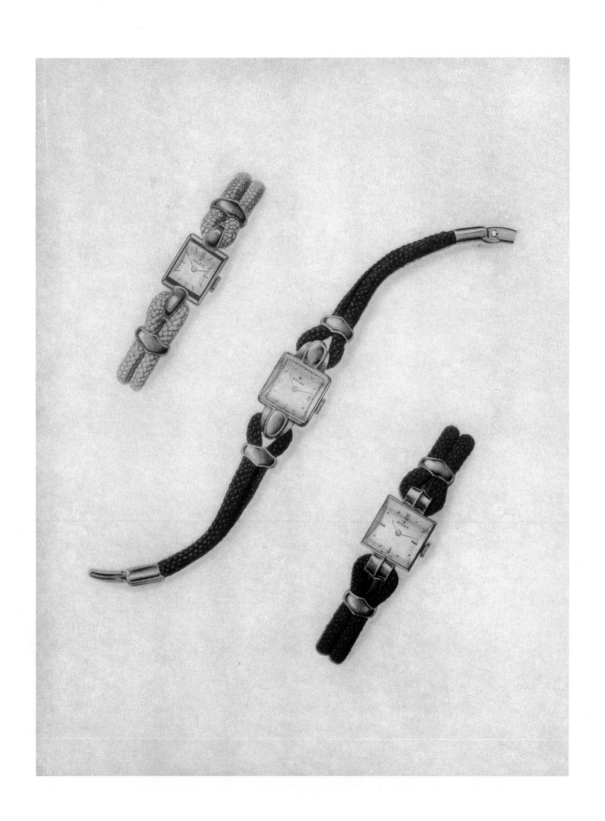

PLATE 16

Ref. 4289   Ref. 4291 (Registered model)   Ref. 4294

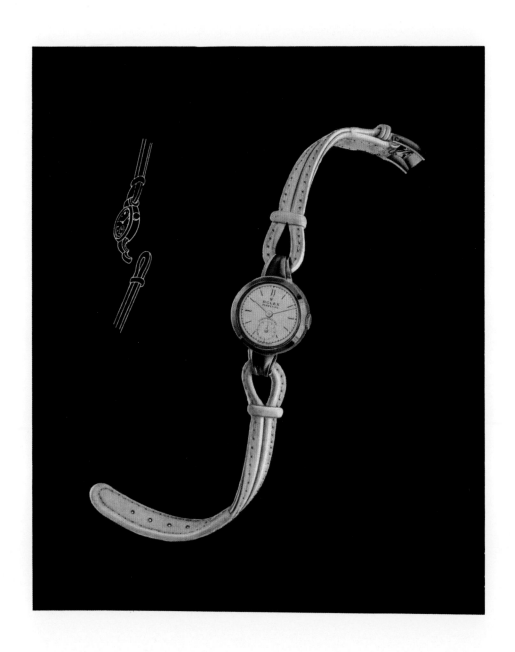

PLATE 17

Ref. 4487 (''Jubilee model'', registered and patented)   87

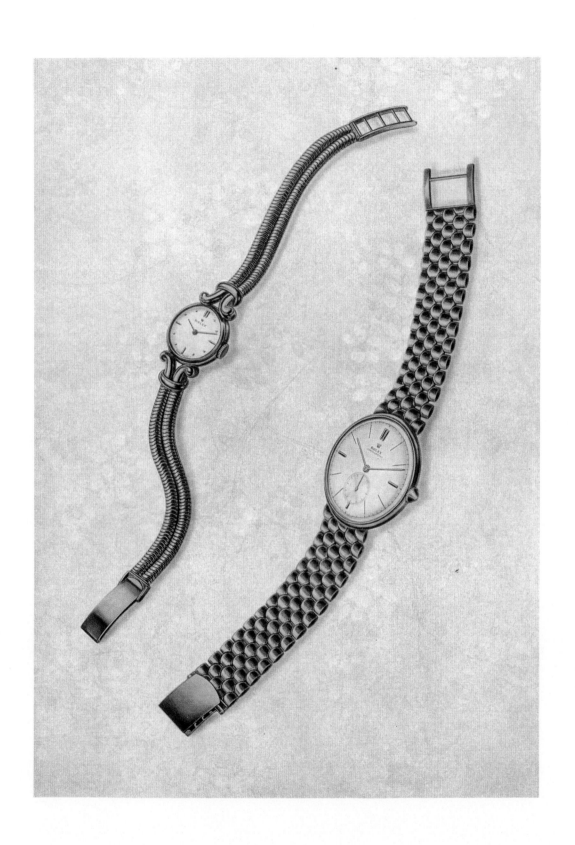

PLATE 18

Ref. 4457 Ref. 4446

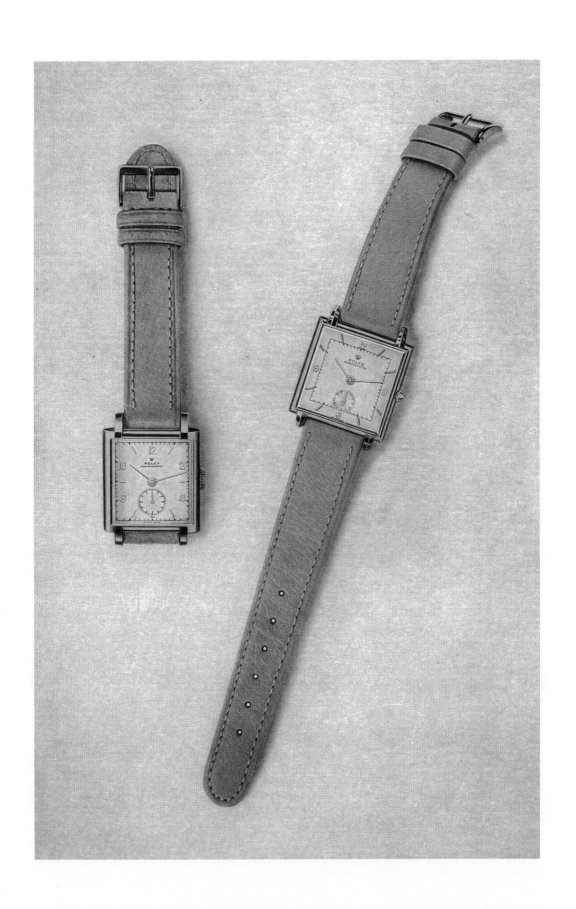

PLATE 20
Ref. 4029 (Registered model)   Ref. 4330

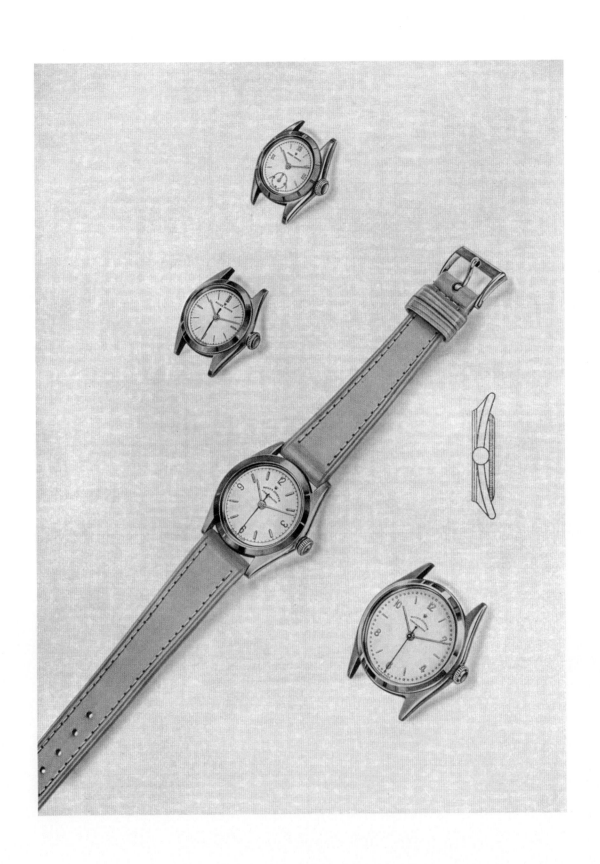

PLATE 21

From top to bottom: Ref. 4437   Ref. 4271   Ref. 4270   Ref. 4365

PLATE 22

Ref. 3923 (Registered model)   Ref. 4364

PLATE 23

From top to bottom: Ref. 4486   Ref. 3772   Ref. 3372/3725 (Registered model)   Ref. 4408

PLATE 24
Ref. 4325 (Registered model)

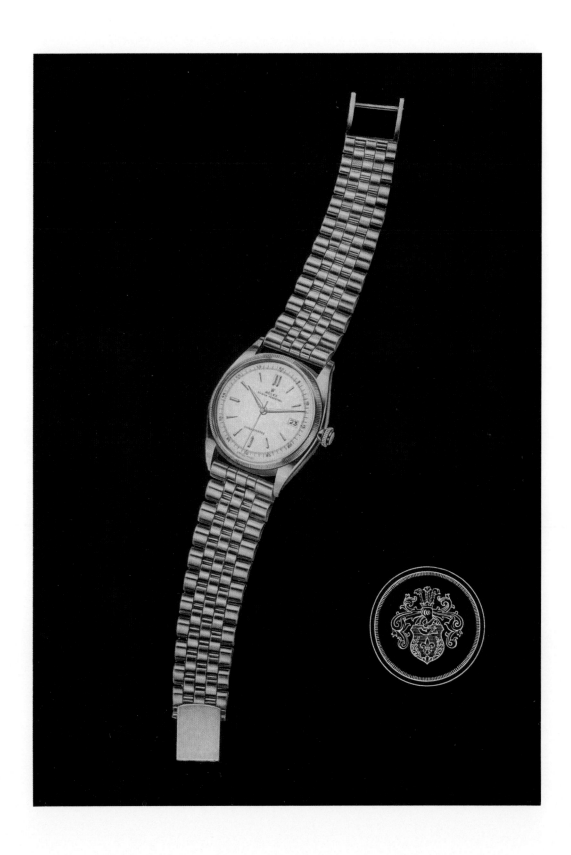

PLATE 25
Ref. 4467 (Registered "Jubilee" model)

PLATE 26
Ref. 4114   Ref. 4262   Ref. 4116

VINTAGE ROLEX WRISTWATCHES

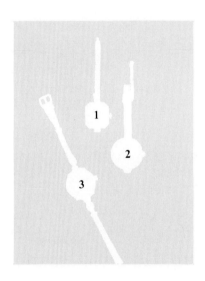

1.
Timeless Elegance ROLEX Ref. No. 262238
Ladies Rolex 18 ct Pink Gold, 1910, Hinged Case,
15 Jewels, W/D Movement, W/D Case, Metal Dial

2.
Timeless Elegance ROLEX Ref. No. 422481
Ladies Rolex 9 ct Pink Gold, 1911, Hinged Case,
15 Jewels Rolex Movement, W/D Case, Enamel Dial

3.
Timeless Elegance ROLEX Ref. No. 248663
Ladies Rolex 9 ct Pink Gold, 1908, Hinged Case,
15 Jewels, X/L Movement, W/D Case, Metal Dial

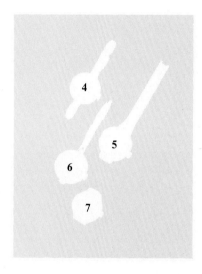

4.
Timeless Elegance ROLEX Ref. No. 445682
Ladies Rolex Hinged Case, 1911, 9 ct Pink Gold,
Case Signed W/D, 15 Jewels, W/D Movement,
Enamel Dial

5.
Timeless Elegance ROLEX Ref. No. 464122
Ladies Rolex Hinged Case, 1911, 9 ct Pink Gold,
Case Signed W/D, Movement Signed W/D, 15 Jewels,
Enamel Dial

6.
Timeless Elegance ROLEX Ref. No. 450321
Ladies Rolex Hinged Case, 1911, 9 ct Pink Gold with Enamel,
Case Signed W/D, X/L Movement, 15 Jewels,
Enamel Dial

7.
Timeless Elegance ROLEX Ref. No. 496435
Ladies Rolex Hinged Case, 1913, 9 ct Pink Gold,
Case Signed W/D, 15 Jewels Movement Signed W/D,
Metal Dial

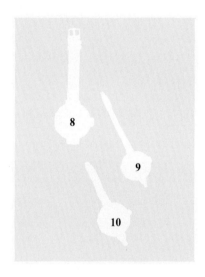

8.
Timeless Elegance ROLEX Ref. No. 746821
Ladies Rolex Hinged Case, 1914, .925 Sterling,
Case Signed W/D, 15 Jewels Rolex Movement,
Enamel Dial

9.
Timeless Elegance ROLEX Ref. No. 810630
Ladies Rolex Half Hunter Hinged Case, 1916, 18 ct Pink Gold,
Case Signed W/D, 15 Jewels Rolex Movement,
Enamel Dial

10.
Timeless Elegance ROLEX Ref. No. 734870
Ladies Rolex Hinged Case, 1912, 9 ct Pink Gold,
Case Signed W/D, 15 Jewels W/D Movement,
Enamel Dial

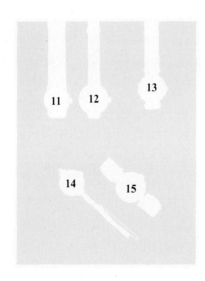

11.
Timeless Elegance ROLEX Ref. No. 3627
Ladies Rolex Hinged Case, 1923, 9 ct Pink Gold,
Case Signed RWC, Rolex 15 Jewels Movement,
Metal Dial

12.
Timeless Elegance ROLEX Ref. No. 698554/4
Ladies Rolex Hinged Case, 1914, .925 Sterling,
Case Signed W/D Rolex, Movement Signed W/D,
Metal Dial

13.
Timeless Elegance ROLEX Ref. No. 3947
Ladies Rolex Hinged Case, 1923, 9 ct Pink Gold,
Case Signed W/D, Movement Signed
Rolwatco 15 Jewels, Metal Dial

14.
Timeless Elegance ROLEX Ref. No. 443322
Ladies Rolex Hinged Case, 1910, 18 ct Yellow Gold + Enamel and Diamonds,
Case Signed W/D, Movement Signed X/L 15 Jewels,
Gold color Metal Dial.

15.
Timeless Elegance ROLEX Ref. No. 484329
Ladies Rolex Hinged Case, 1912, 18 ct Pink Gold with Enamel,
Case Signed W/D, Movement Signed W/D 15 Jewels,
Gold Color Metal Dial

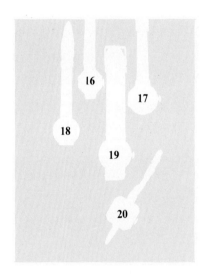

16.
Timeless Elegance ROLEX Ref. No. 128644/14
Ladies Rolex Hinged Case, 1930, 18 ct White Gold,
Case Signed Rolex 7 World's Record's,
Movement Rolex Ultra Prima 15 Jewels,
Gold Color Metal Dial

17.
Timeless Elegance ROLEX Ref. No. 572794
Ladies Rolex Hinged Case, 1914, 9 ct Pink Gold With Enamel,
Case Signed W/D, Rolex 15 Jewels Movement,
White Metal Dial

18.
Timeless Elegance ROLEX Ref. No. 458392
Ladies Rolex Two Piece Case, 1937, 9 ct Yellow Gold,
Case Signed Rolex 25 World's Record's,
Movement 15 Jewels Rolex Precision, White Metal Dial

19.
Timeless Elegance ROLEX Ref. No. 22331
Ladies Rolex Hinged Case, 1927, 9 ct Pink Gold,
Case Signed Rolex 7 World's Records
Gold-Medal Geneve-Suisse RWC LTD,
Rolex 15 Jewels Movement,
White Metal Dial

20.
Timeless Elegance ROLEX Ref. No. 149356
Ladies Rolex Hinged Case, 1920, 9 ct Pink Gold,
Case Signed W/D Swiss, Rolex 15 Jewels
Movement, Gold Color Metal Dial

21.
Timeless Elegance ROLEX Ref. No. 8892
Ladies Rolex Hinged Case, 1924, 9 ct Pink Gold,
Case Signed RWC, Rolex 15 Jewels Movement,
Enamel Dial

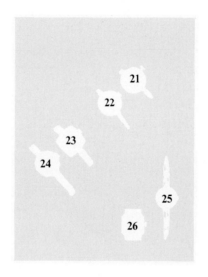

22.
Timeless Elegance ROLEX Ref. No. 22377
Ladies Rolex Hinged Case, 1912, 9 ct Pink Gold,
Case Signed W/D, Rolex 15 Jewels Movement,
Metal Dial

23.
Timeless Elegance ROLEX Ref. No. 31240
Ladies Rolex Hinged Case, 1926, 9 ct Pink Gold,
Case Signed RWC, Rolex 15 Jewels Movement,
Enamel Dial

24.
Timeless Elegance ROLEX Ref. No. 29437
Ladies Rolex Hinged Case, 1922, 9 ct Pink Gold,
Case Signed W/D, Rolex 15 Jewels Movement,
Metal Dial

25.
Timeless Elegance ROLEX Ref. No. 1050P/68124
Ladies Rolex Hinged Case, 1924, 9 ct Pink Gold,
Case Signed RWC, Rolex 15 Rubies Standard Quality,
Metal Dial

26.
Timeless Elegance ROLEX Ref. No. 1143138
Ladies Rolex Hinged Case, 1920, 9 ct Two Color White + Yellow Gold,
Case Signed W/D, Genex Veriflat 15 Jewels Movement,
Metal Dial

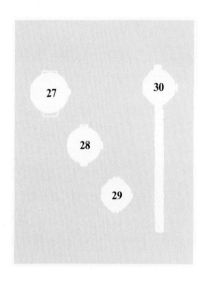

27.
Timeless Elegance ROLEX Ref. No. 580135
Ladies Rolex Hinged Case, 1914, 9 ct Pink Gold,
Case Signed W/D, Rolex 15 Jewels Movement,
Enamel Dial

28.
Timeless Elegance ROLEX Ref. No. 37509
Ladies Rolex Hinged Case, 1926, 9 ct Pink Gold,
Case Signed RWC, Rolex 15 Rubies Movement,
Enamel Dial

29.
Timeless Elegance ROLEX Ref. No. 90/506212
Ladies Rolex Hinged Case, 1915, 9 ct Pink Gold,
Case Signed RWC, Rolco 15 Jewels #200 Movement,
Metal Dial

30.
Timeless Elegance ROLEX Ref. No. 1084723
Ladies Rolex Hinged Case, 1919, 18 ct Yellow Gold,
Case Signed W/D Rolex, Movement Signed Rolex 15 Jewels,
Metal Dial

31.
Timeless Elegance ROLEX Ref. No. 31248
Ladies Rolex Hinged Case, 1925, 9 ct Pink Gold,
Case Signed RWC 7 World's Record's, Rolex 15 Jewels Movement,
Metal Dial

32.
Timeless Elegance ROLEX Ref. No. 8901
Ladies Rolex Hinged Case, 1924, 9 ct Pink Gold,
Case Signed RWC 7 World's Record's, Rolex 15 Jewels Movement,
Metal Dial

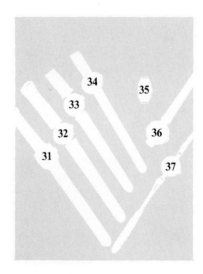

33.
Timeless Elegance ROLEX Ref. No. 12557/013
Ladies Hinged Case, 1924, 9 ct Pink Gold,
Case Signed RWC, 15 Jewels Rolex Movement,
Metal Dial

34.
Timeless Elegance ROLEX Ref. No. 104414
Ladies Rolex Hinged Case, 1926, 9 ct Pink Gold,
Case Signed RWC LTD, 15 Jewels Rolex Movement,
Metal Dial

35.
Timeless Elegance ROLEX Ref. No. 69397/1375A
Ladies Rolex Two Piece Case, 1930, 9 ct Pink Gold,
Case Signed Rolex 25 World's Record's, 15 Rubies Rolex Prima Movement,
Timed 6 Positions Rolex Hairspring,
Metal Dial

36.
Timeless Elegance ROLEX Ref. No. 521789
Ladies Rolex Hinged Case, 1913, 9 ct Pink Gold + Enamel,
Case Signed W/D, 15 Jewels Rolex Movement,
Metal Dial

37.
Timeless Elegance ROLEX Ref. No. 1158958
Ladies Rolex Half Hunter, 1927, 9 ct Pink Gold,
Case Signed W/D, 15 Jewels Rolex Movement,
Enamel Dial

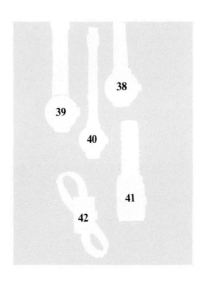

38.
Timeless Elegance ROLEX Ref. No. 101421
Ladies Rolex Hinged Case, 1925, 9 ct Two Color Pink + Yellow,
Case Signed RWC, Rolex 15 Jewels Movement, Metal Dial

39.
Timeless Elegance ROLEX Ref. No. 104111
Ladies Rolex Hinged Case, 1926, 9 ct Pink Gold,
Case Signed RWC, Rolex 15 Jewels Movement, Metal Dial

40.
Timeless Elegance ROLEX Ref. No. 98741
Ladies Rolex Hinged Case, 1924, 9 ct Pink Gold,
Case Signed RWC, Rolex 15 Jewels Movement, Metal Dial

41.
Timeless Elegance ROLEX Ref. No. 110641
Men's Rolex Hinged case Moveable Lugs, 1929, 9 ct Yellow Gold,
Case Signed RWC, Rolex 15 Jewels Movement, Metal Dial

42.
Timeless Elegance ROLEX Ref. No. 108421
Ladies Rolex Hinged Case, 1928, 9 ct Yellow Gold,
Case Signed RWC, Rolex 15 Jewels Movement, Metal Dial

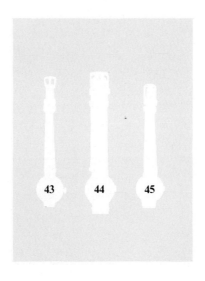

43.
Timeless Elegance ROLEX Ref. No. 11287
Ladies's Rolex Hinged Case, 1924, 9 ct Pink Gold,
Case Signed RWC 7 World's Record's, Rolex 15 Jewels
Timed For Six Positions And For All Climates on Movement, Metal Dial

44.
Timeless Elegance ROLEX Ref. No. 29705
Men's Rolex Hinged case, 1922, 9 ct Pink Gold,
Case Signed W/D, Rolex 15 Jewels Movement, Metal Dial

45.
Timeless Elegance ROLEX Ref. No. 1047A/73155
Ladies Rolex Hinged Case, 1930, 9 ct Pink Gold,
Case Signed Rolex 25 World's Record's,
Rolex Marconi 15 Jewels Movement,
Metal Dial

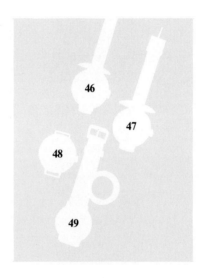

46.
Timeless Elegance ROLEX Ref. No. 784937
Men's Rolex Half Hunter, 1919, .925 Sterling,
Case Signed W/D Swiss made, 15 Jewels Rolex Movement, Enamel Dial

47.
Timeless Elegance ROLEX Ref. No. 774070
Men's Rolex Full Hunter, 1917, .925 Sterling
Case Signed W/D, 15 Jewels Rolex Movement, Enamel Dial

48.
Timeless Elegance ROLEX Ref. No. 10183
Men's Rolex Three Piece Case, 1917, .925 Sterling
Case Signed JF, 15 Jewels Swiss made Rolex Movement, Enamel Dial

49.
Timeless Elegance ROLEX Ref. No. 356
Men's Rolex Five Piece Case, 1920, 9 ct Pink Gold,
Case Signed SAB Bangkok Rolex, 15 Jewels Movement, Enamel Dial

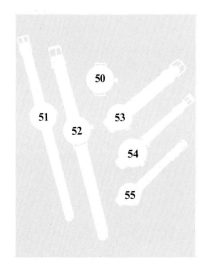

50.
Timeless Elegance ROLEX Ref. No. 332
Men's Rolex Three Piece Case, 1912, Gun metal,
Case Signed W/D Rolex, 15 Jewels Rolex Movement, Enamel Dial

51.
Timeless Elegance ROLEX Ref. No. 625871
Men's Rolex Hinged Case, 1934, 9 ct Pink Gold,
Case Signed W/D Swiss made, 15 Jewels, Enamel Dial

52.
Timeless Elegance ROLEX Ref. No. 996865
Men's Rolex Three Piece Case, 1918 Sterling + Gold,
Case Signed W/D Swiss, 15 Jewels Rolex Movement, Enamel Dial

53.
Timeless Elegance ROLEX Ref. No. 101693
Men's Rolex Hinged Case, 1925, 9 ct Pink Gold,
Case Signed RWC LTD, 15 Jewels Rolex Movement, Metal Dial

54.
Timeless Elegance ROLEX Ref. No. 80824
Men's Rolex Half Hunter, 1924, .925 Sterling,
Case Signed W/D Rolex Swiss, 15 Jewels Rolex Movement, Enamel Dial

55.
Timeless Elegance ROLEX Ref. No. 1076484
Ladies Rolex Hinged Case, 1936, .925 Sterling,
Case Signed Rolex Swiss W/D, 15 Jewels Rolex Movement, Enamel Dial

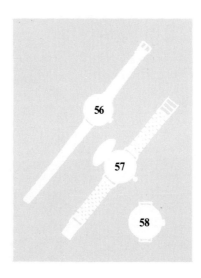

56.
Timeless Elegance ROLEX Ref. No. 188750
Men's Rolex Hinged Case, 1932, 9 ct Pink Gold
Case Signed RWC, Unicorn Movement 15 Jewels, Enamel Dial

57.
Timeless Elegance ROLEX Ref. No. 222823
Men's Rolex Half Hunter, 1919, 9 ct Yellow Gold
Case Signed ALD, Rolex Movement 15 Jewels, Enamel Dial

58.
Timeless Elegance ROLEX Ref. No. 807281
Men's Rolex Half Hunter, 1924, .925 Sterling
Case Signed W/D, 15 Jewels Rolex Movement, Enamel Dial

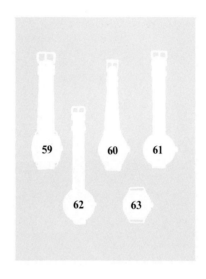

59.
Timeless Elegance ROLEX Ref. No. 3654
Men's Rolex Three Piece Case, 1917, .925 Sterling,
Case Signed W/D, Rolex 15 Jewels Movement, Enamel Dial

60.
Timeless Elegance ROLEX Ref. No. 104099/81
Men's Rolex Three Piece Case, 1908, .925 Sterling,
Case Signed RWC, Rolex Dunklings Movement,
15 Jewels, Enamel Dial

61.
Timeless Elegance ROLEX Ref. No. 220/1111
Men's Rolex Three Piece Case, 1915, .925 Sterling
Case Signed Rolex, 15 Jewels Rolex Movement, Metal Dial

62.
Timeless Elegance ROLEX Ref. No. 826791
Men's Rolex Hinged Case, 1918, 925 Sterling,
Case Signed W/D, Rolex 15 Jewels Movement, Metal Dial

63.
Timeless Elegance ROLEX Ref. No. 107384/178
Men's Rolex Three Piece Case, 1927, 925 Sterling,
Case Signed RWC LTD, Unicorn 15 Jewels Movement, Metal Dial

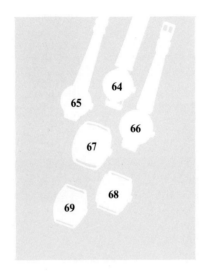

64.
Timeless Elegance ROLEX Ref. No. 14588
Men's Rolex Hinged Case, 1921, 18 ct Yellow Gold,
Case Signed Dennison, Rolex 15 Jewels Movement, Metal Dial

65.
Timeless Elegance ROLEX Ref. No. 12568
Ladies Rolex Hinged Case, 1924, 9 ct Pink Gold,
Case Signed RWC LTD, Rolex 15 Jewels Movement, Enamel Dial

66.
Timeless Elegance ROLEX Ref. No. 14061
Ladies Rolex Hinged Case, 1925, 9 ct Pink Gold,
Case Signed RWC, Rolex 15 Jewels Movement, Metal Dial

67.
Timeless Elegance ROLEX Ref. No. 65222
Men's Rolex Three Piece Case, 1925, 9 ct Yellow Gold,
Case Signed Dennison, Rolex 15 Jewels Movement, Enamel Dial

68.
Timeless Elegance ROLEX Ref. No. 13851
Men's Rolex Oyster Two Piece Case, 1925, 9 ct Yellow Gold,
Case Signed RWC, Rolex 15 Jewels Movement, Metal Dial

69.
Timeless Elegance ROLEX Ref. No. 111423
Men's Rolex Two Piece Case, 1924, 9 ct Pink Gold,
Case Signed RWC, Rolex 15 Jewels Movement, Metal Dial

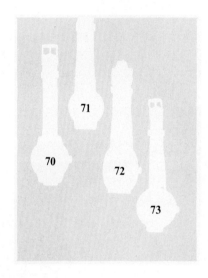

70.
Timeless Elegance ROLEX Ref. No. 50125
Men's Rolex Two Piece Case, 1924, .925 Sterling,
Case Signed Rolex 7 World's Record's, Rolex 15 Jewels Movement, Enamel Dial

71.
Timeless Elegance ROLEX Ref. No. 356
Men's Rolex Five Piece Case, 1924, 9 ct Pink Gold,
Case Signed RWC, Rolex 15 Jewels Movement, Enamel Dial

72.
Timeless Elegance ROLEX Ref. No. 65432
Men's Rolex Three Piece Case, 1926, Gold Filled,
Case Signed Dennison 20 yrs, Rolex 15 Jewels Movement, Enamel Dial

73.
Timeless Elegance ROLEX Ref. No. 786431
Men's Rolex Half Hunter, 1921, .925 Sterling,
Case Signed W/D Rolex, Rolex 15 Jewels Movement, Enamel Dial

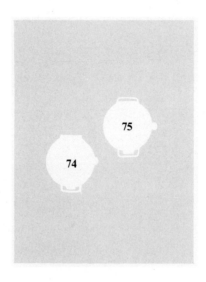

74.
Timeless Elegance ROLEX Ref. No. 974416
Men's Rolex Full Hunter, 1919, 18K Yellow Gold,
Case Signed W/D Swiss made, 15 Jewels Rolex Movement, Enamel Dial

75.
Timeless Elegance ROLEX Ref. No. 974409
Men's Rolex Half Hunter, 1919, 18K Yellow Gold,
Case Signed W/D Swiss made, 15 Jewels Rolex Movement, Enamel Dial

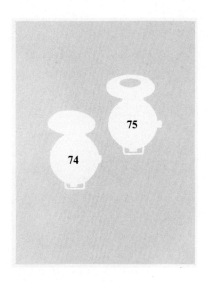

74.
Timeless Elegance ROLEX Ref. No. 974416
Open view

75.
Timeless Elegance ROLEX Ref. No. 974409
Open view

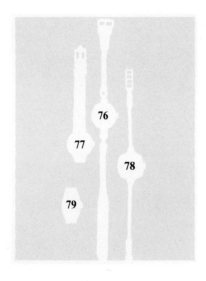

76.
Timeless Elegance ROLEX Ref. No. 21882/2522
Ladies Rolex 9 ct Pink Gold, 1937,
Two Piece Case, 15 Rubies Rolex Prima, Subsidiary Seconds Hand,
Case, Dial, Movement Signed Rolex

77.
Timeless Elegance ROLEX Ref. No. 34521/178
Ladies Rolex 9 ct Pink Gold, 1923, Hinged Case,
15 Jewels Rolex Marconi Movement, Two Tone Dial, Case Dial Movement Signed Rolex

78.
Timeless Elegance ROLEX Ref. No. 23946/2618
Ladies Rolex 9 ct Pink Gold, 1939,
Two Piece Case 15 Rubies Rolex Prima Movement, Subsidiary Seconds Hand,
Case, Dial, Movement Signed Rolex

79.
Timeless Elegance ROLEX Ref. No. 1252/452
Ladies Rolex 9 ct Pink Gold, 1933,
Two Piece Case, 15 Jewels, Prima 6 Positions, Silver Dial,
Case, Dial, Movement Signed Rolex

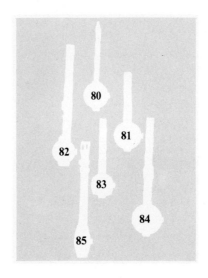

80.
Timeless Elegance ROLEX Ref. No. 11288
Ladies Rolex 9 ct Pink Gold, 1924,
Hinged Case, Subsidiary Seconds Hand, 7 World's Records RWC Signed Case,
15 Jewels, Timed 6 Position for All Climates
Dial, Movement Signed Rolex

81.
Timeless Elegance ROLEX Ref. No. 29522
Ladies Rolex 18 ct Pink Gold, 1922, Hinged Case,
15 Jewels Rolex Movement and Dial, W/D Case

82.
Timeless Elegance ROLEX Ref. No. 110226
Ladies Rolex 9 ct Pink Gold, 1927, Hinged Case,
15 Jewels, RWC LTD, Dial, Movement Signed Rolex

83.
Timeless Elegance ROLEX Ref. No. 42861
Ladies Rolex 9 ct Pink Gold, 1928, Hinged Case,
15 Jewels, 7 World's Records, RWC Signed Case, Dial, Movement Signed Rolex

84.
Timeless Elegance ROLEX Ref. No. 576231
Ladies Rolex 18 ct Pink Gold, 1914, Hinged Case,
15 Jewels Rolex Movement and Dial, W/D Case

85.
Timeless Elegance ROLEX Ref. No. 412226
Ladies Rolex 9 ct Pink Gold, 1927, Two Piece Case,
17 Jewel Prima Movement,
Dial, Case, Movement Signed Rolex

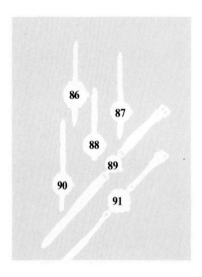

86.
Timeless Elegance ROLEX Ref. No. 9206
Ladies Rolex 9 ct Pink Gold, 1925,
Hinged Case, RWC 7 World's Record's, 15 Jewels, Dial, Case, Movement Signed Rolex

87.
Timeless Elegance ROLEX Ref. No. 26478
Ladies Rolex 9 ct Pink Gold, 1924,
Hinged Case, 15 Jewels Timed 6 Position, For All Climates,
7 World's Record's, Case, Dial, Movement Signed Rolex

88.
Timeless Elegance ROLEX Ref. No. 510622
Ladies Rolex 9 ct Pink Gold, 1912,
Hinged Case, 15 Jewels Rolex Movement and Dial, W/D Case

89.
Timeless Elegance ROLEX Ref. No. 14265/027
Ladies Rolex 9 ct Pink Gold, 1924,
Hinged Case, 15 Jewels Rolex Movement and Dial, Case Signed RWC

90.
Timeless Elegance ROLEX Ref. No. 27285
Ladies Rolex 9 ct Pink Gold, 1921,
Hinged Case, 15 Jewels Rolex Movement,
Rolex Metal Dial, W/D Case

91.
Timeless Elegance ROLEX Ref. No. 317286
Ladies Rolex 9 ct, Pink Gold, 1941, Two Piece Case made by B + S for Rolex Precision,
17 Rubies Rolex Movement

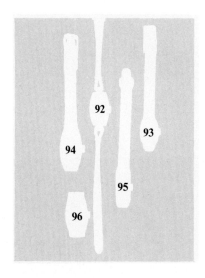

92.
Timeless Elegance ROLEX Ref. No. 1286
Ladies Rolex Two Piece Case, 1933, 9 ct Yellow Gold,
Case Signed RWC, Rolex 15 Jewels Movement, Metal Dial

93.
Timeless Elegance ROLEX Ref. No. 1854
Ladies Rolex Two Piece Case, 1936, 18 ct Yellow Gold,
Case Signed RWC, Rolex 15 Jewels Movement, Metal Dial

94.
Timeless Elegance ROLEX Ref. No. 1324
Ladies Rolex Two Piece Case, 1934, 9 ct Pink Gold,
Case Signed RWC, Rolex 15 Jewels Movement, Metal Dial

95.
Timeless Elegance ROLEX Ref. No. 1367
Ladies Rolex Princess, 1934, 18 ct White Gold,
Case Signed RWC, Rolex Princess 15 Jewels Movement, Metal Dial

96.
Timeless Elegance ROLEX Ref. No. 2014
Ladies Rolex Two Piece Case, 1937, 9 ct Two Color White + Pink,
Case Signed RWC, Rolex 15 Jewels Movement, Metal Dial

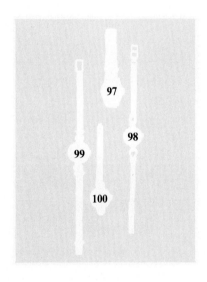

97.
Timeless Elegance ROLEX Ref. No. 22648/2611
Ladies Rolex 9 ct Pink Gold, 1938, Two Piece Case,
17 Jewels, Subsidiary Seconds Hand, Case, Dial, Movement Signed Rolex

98.
Timeless Elegance ROLEX Ref. No. 49862
Ladies Rolex 18 ct Pink Gold, 1936, Two Piece Case, 17 Jewel, For All Climates, Prima Movement,
Case, Dial, Movement Signed Rolex

99.
Timeless Elegance ROLEX Ref. No. 49238
Ladies Rolex 18 ct Pink Gold 1935, Two Piece Case, 17 Jewel 6 Position Movement,
Case, Dial, Movement Signed Rolex

100.
Timeless Elegance ROLEX Ref. No. 26311/2636
Ladies Rolex 9 ct Pink Gold, 1940,
Two Piece Case, Subsidiary Seconds Hand, 17 Jewels Extra Prima Movement,
Case, Dial, Movement Signed Rolex

101.
Timeless Elegance ROLEX Ref. No. 247
Ladies Rolex Sterling Silver and Enamel,1910,
Elongated Three Piece Case, Enamel Dial,
W/D Movement W/D Case, Rolex on Dial

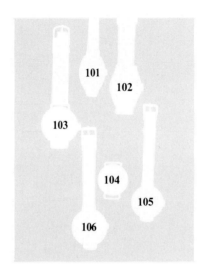

102.
Timeless Elegance ROLEX Ref. No. 30223/2942
Men's Rolex 18 ct Pink Gold, 1936,
Three Piece Case, Enamel Dial, Sweep Seconds Hand,
Dial, Case, Movement Signed Rolex

103.
Timeless Elegance ROLEX Ref. No. 894162
Men's Rolex Sterling Silver, 1917,
Round Three Piece Case, Subsidiary Seconds, Enamel Dial, Signed W/D Movement Rolex Case

104.
Timeless Elegance ROLEX Ref. No. 1865/356
Men's Rolex 18 ct Yellow Gold, 1921,
Early Water Resistent 4 Piece Case, Screw Bezel,
Subsidiary Seconds W/D Case, Rolex Movement

105.
Timeless Elegance ROLEX Ref. No. 778182
Men's Rolex Sterling Silver. Half Hunter, 1917,
Enamel Dial, Hinged Case, Signed W/D, Rolex Movement

106.
Timeless Elegance ROLEX Ref. No. 974254
Men's Rolex 9 ct Pink Gold, 1917,
Round Two Piece Case,
Enamel Dial, Subsidiary Seconds, W/D Case, Rolex Movement

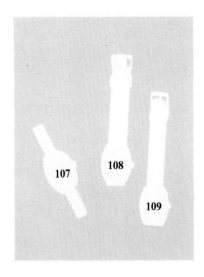

107.
Timeless Elegance ROLEX Ref. No. 38174
Men's Rolex Two Piece Case, 1923, 9 ct Pink Gold,
Case Signed Rolex 28 World's Record's, Rolex Prima Movement 15 Rubies,
Two Tone Metal Dial Signed Rolex

108.
Timeless Elegance ROLEX Ref. No. 341
Men's Rolex Two Piece Case, 1924, 9 ct Pink Gold,
Case Signed Rolex 7 World's Record's, Rolex 15 Jewels Movement,
Engraved of on Back OW to JFC 24-11-25, Enamel Dial

109.
Timeless Elegance ROLEX Ref. No. 41687/554
Men's Rolex Curved Back Two Piece Case, 1927, 9 ct Pink Gold,
Case Signed RWC, Rolex Prima 15 Jewels Movement,
Metal Dial

110.
Timeless Elegance ROLEX Ref. No. 907
Men's Rolex Oyster Case, 1927, 925 Silver + 9 ct Gold,
Case Signed RWC, Rolex 15 Jewels,
Prima Movement, 16 World's Record's,
Metal Dial

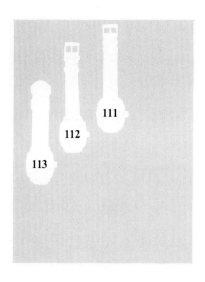

111.
Timeless Elegance ROLEX Ref. No. 36124/2081
Men's Rolex Oyster Case, 1938, 9 ct Two Color White + Pink,
Case Signed Rolex, 15 Jewels Swiss Made Movement,
Metal Dial

112.
Timeless Elegance ROLEX Ref. No. 4163/678
Men's Rolex Oyster Case, 1927, .925 Sterling,
Case Signed RWC, Rolex 15 Jewels Rolex Movement,
Metal Dial.

113.
Timeless Elegance ROLEX Ref. No. 74164/2190
Men's Rolex Oyster Case, 1932, Chrome Plated,
Case Signed Oyster Watch Company,
Rolex 15 Jewels Movement,
Enamel Dial

114.
Timeless Elegance ROLEX Ref. No. 27305/678
Men's Rolex Oyster Case, 1931, 9 ct Pink Gold,
Subsidiary Seconds, Case Signed RWC, Rolex 15 Rubies Movement,
Metal Dial

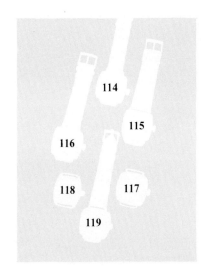

115.
Timeless Elegance ROLEX Ref. No. 28461/678
Men's Rolex Oyster Case, 1932, 18 ct Pink Gold,
Subsidiary Seconds, Case Signed RWC 20 World's Record's,
17 Jewels Super Balance Rolex Extra Prima Movement,
Metal Dial

116.
Timeless Elegance ROLEX Ref. No. 471002/678
Men's Rolex Oyster Case, 1933, Pink Gold,
Subsidiary Seconds, Case Signed RWC Oyster Watch Company,
17 Jewels Super Balance Rolex Movement,
Metal Dial

117.
Timeless Elegance ROLEX Ref. No. 27154/678
Men's Rolex Oyster Case, 1930, 9 ct Yellow Gold,
Subsidiary Seconds, Case Signed RWC, Rolex 15 Jewels Ultra Prima Movement,
Enamel Dial

118.
Timeless Elegance ROLEX Ref. No. 25255/714
Men's Rolex Oyster Case, 1930, 9 ct Pink Gold,
Subsidiary Seconds, Case Signed RWC 20 World's Record's,
15 Rubies 6 Position Rolex Movement,
Metal Dial

119.
Timeless Elegance ROLEX Ref. No. 29932/678
Men's Rolex Oyster Case, 1933, 9 ct Pink Gold,
Subsidiary Seconds, Case Signed RWC Oyster Watch Company,
Rolex 17 Jewels Super Balance,
Metal Dial

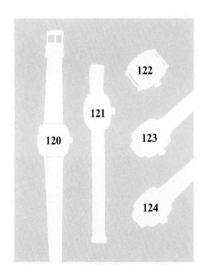

120.
Timeless Elegance ROLEX Ref. No. 18761/678
Men's Rolex Oyster Case, 1928, 9 ct Pink Gold,
Center Sweep Hand, Case Signed RWC, Rolex 15 Jewels Movement,
Metal Dial, Center Sweep Hand

121.
Timeless Elegance ROLEX Ref. No. 24266/713
Ladies Rolex Oyster Case, 1927, 9 ct Pink Gold,
Subsidiary Seconds, Case Signed RWC, Rolex 15 Jewels Movement,
Metal Dial

122.
Timeless Elegance ROLEX Ref. No. 57015/678
Men's Rolex Oyster Case, 1929, Chrome,
Subsidiary Seconds, Case Signed SAR Oyster Watch Company,
Rolco Movement 15 Jewels,
Metal Dial

123.
Timeless Elegance ROLEX Ref. No. 21029/678
Men's Rolex Oyster Case, 1936, 9 ct Pink Gold,
Subsidiary Seconds, Case Signed ROLEX 20 World's Record's
Movement Signed Rolex 15 Jewels,
Metal Dial.

124.
Timeless Elegance ROLEX Ref. No. 28918/678
Men's Rolex Oyster Case, 1932, 9 ct Pink Gold,
Subsidiary Seconds, Case Signed RWC 20 World's Record's,
Movement Signed Rolex Ultra Prima 6 Position 15 Jewels,
Metal Dial

125.
Timeless Elegance ROLEX Ref. No. 32419/2546
Men's Rolex 9 ct, Pink Gold, 1935, with Hooded Two Piece Case,
Subsidiary Seconds, Metal Dial,
18 Rubies Ultra Prima, Chronometer, RWC, Case, Movement, Dial Signed Rolex

126.
Timeless Elegance ROLEX Ref. No. 95300F/2136
Men's Rolex Stainless Steel, and Pink Gold Bezel, 1932,
Octagonal Oyster, Three Piece Case, Subsidiary Seconds, Metal Dial
17 Rubies, Ultra Prima Super Balance, Case, Dial, Movement Signed Rolex

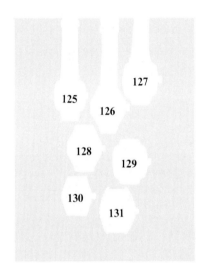

127.
Timeless Elegance ROLEX Ref. No. 28411/678
Men's Rolex 18 ct Pink Gold, 1930, Cushion Oyster,
Subsidiary Seconds, Enamel Dial, Three Piece Case,
15 Jewels, Ultra Prima, Movement, Dial, Case Signed Rolex

128.
Timeless Elegance ROLEX Ref. No. 27415
Men's Rolex 9 ct Pink Gold, 1929, Octangonal Oyster, Subsidiary Second,
Three Piece Case, Metal Dial, 15 Jewels, Prima Super Balance, Case, Dial, Movement Signed Rolex

129.
Timeless Elegance ROLEX Ref. No. 29442/678
Men's Rolex 9 ct Yellow Gold, 1931, Cushion Oyster, Enamel Dial,
Subsidiary Seconds, Three Piece Case, 17 Jewels, Ultra Prima, Case Dial, Movement Signed Rolex

130.
Timeless Elegance ROLEX Ref. No. 39822/2595
Men's Rolex 18 ct Yellow Gold, 1934, Oyster Two Piece Case, Subsidiary Seconds, Metal Dial,
17 Jewels, Case, Dial, Movement Signed Rolex

131.
Timeless Elegance ROLEX Ref. No. 66826/678
Men's Rolex 18 ct Yellow and White Gold, Cured Sides, 1938,
Oyster Three Piece Case, Subsidiary Seconds, Metal Dial,
17 Jewels, Extra Prima 6 Position, Case, Movement, Dial Signed Rolex

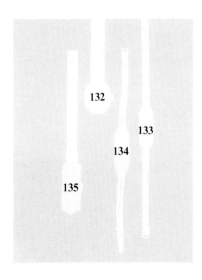

132.
Timeless Elegance ROLEX Ref. No. 34599/015
Ladies Rolex Hinged Case, 1926, 18 ct Yellow Gold and Diamonds,
Case Signed Rolex 7 World's Records,
Gold-Medal Geneve-Suisse RWC LTD,
Rolex Prima Timed 6 Positions for All Climates 15 Jewels Movement,
White Metal Dial

133.
Timeless Elegance ROLEX Ref. No. 3626/1477
Ladies Rolex Hinged Case, 1927, Platium with Diamonds,
Case Signed RWC LTD, Rolex Princess 15 Jewels Movement,
White Metal Dial

134.
Timeless Elegance ROLEX Ref. No. 5317/1406
Ladies Rolex Two Piece Case, 1929, 18 ct White Gold with Diamonds,
Case Signed RWC LTD, Rolex Princess 15 Jewels Movement,
Gold Metal Dial

135.
Timeless Elegance ROLEX Ref. No. 46521
Ladies Rolex Hinged Case, 1923, 18 ct White Gold and Diamonds,
Case Signed RWC LTD, Rolex 15 Jewels Movement,
White Metal Dial

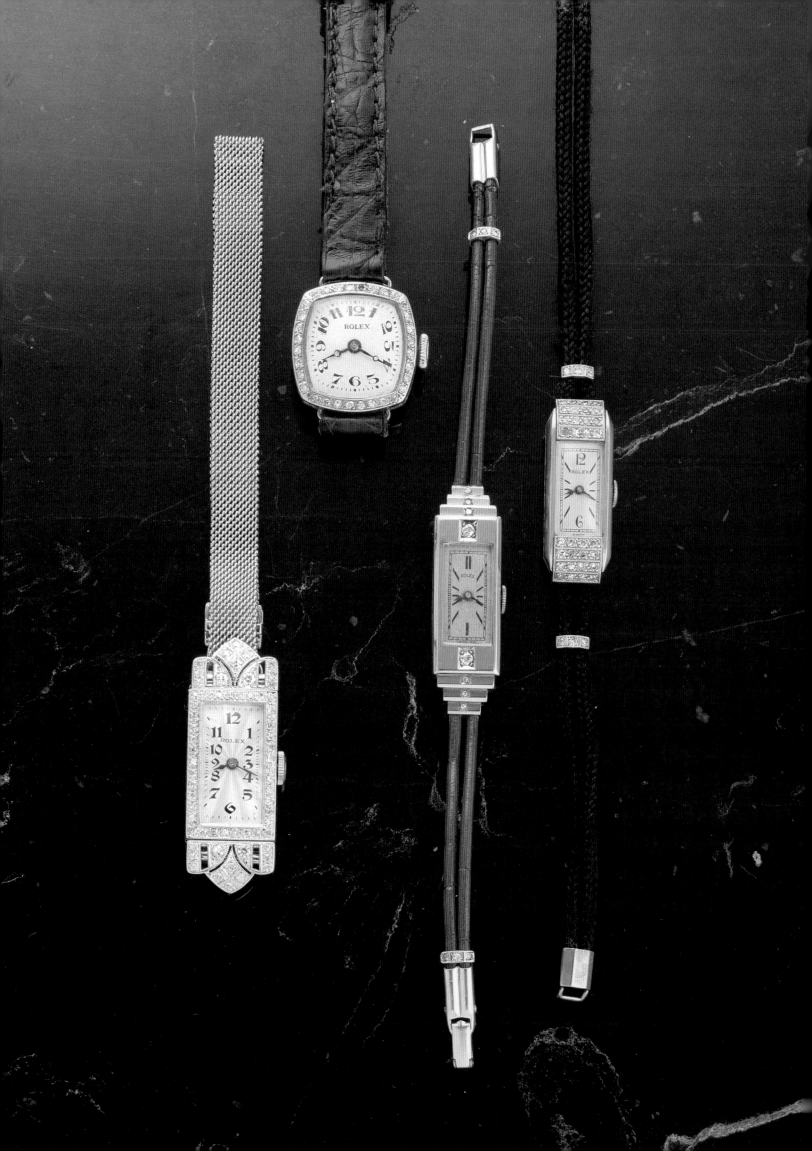

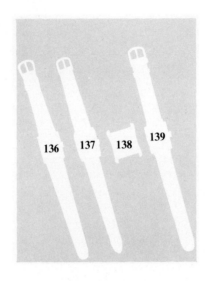

136.
Timeless Elegance ROLEX Ref. No. 60503/332
Men's Rolex Hinged Case, 1927, 18 ct Pink Gold,
Case Signed Rolex 7 World's Record's
Gold-Medal Geneva-Suisse RWC LTD,
Rolex 15 Jewels 6 Positions Movement,
White Metal Dial

137.
Timeless Elegance ROLEX Ref. No. 124799/677
Men's Rolex Hinged Case, 1929, 9 ct Yellow Gold,
Case Signed RWC LTD,
Movement Marconi Rolex 15 Rubies Swiss,
White Metal Dial

138.
Timeless Elegance ROLEX Ref. No. 252
Men's Rolex Two Piece Case 1955, 9 ct Pink + White Gold,
Case Signed RCW LTD, Rolco 15 Jewels Swiss Made Movement,
White Metal Dial

139.
Timeless Elegance ROLEX Ref. No. 38076/6
Men's Rolex Hinged Case, 1927, 18 ct Pink Gold,
Case Signed Rolex 7 World's Record's
Gold-Medal Geneva-Suisse RWC LTD,
Movement Signed Rolex Ultra Prima
Timed 6 Position 15 Rubies Elinvar Hair Spring,
White Metal Dial

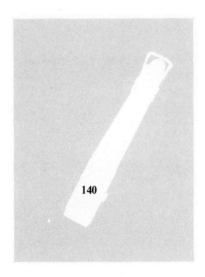

140.
Timeless Elegance ROLEX Ref. No. 9957/1599
Men's Rolex Two Piece Prince Case, 1931, 9 ct Pink Gold,
Case Signed RWC LTD, ROLEX Prince Precision
Antimagnetic Extra Prima 6 Positions Rolex Hairspring Observatory Quality Movement,
Two Tone Metal Dial

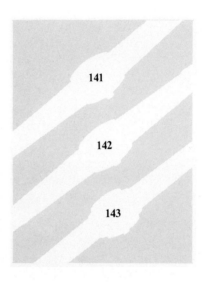

141.
Timeless Elegance ROLEX Ref. No. 73418/1394
Men's Rolex Hinged Case, 1930, 9 ct Yellow Gold,
Case Signed RWC, 15 Rubies Super Balance Rolex Movement,
White Metal Dial

142.
Timeless Elegance ROLEX Ref. No. 73445/1394
Men's Rolex Hinged Case, 1930, 9 ct Pink Gold,
Case Signed RWC, 15 Rubies 6 Positions Extra Prima Rolex Movement,
White Metal Dial

143.
Timeless Elegance ROLEX Ref. No. 47118/3428
Men's Rolex Two Piece Case, 1938, 9 ct Yellow Gold,
Case Signed Rolex S.A., 15 Jewels 6 Position for All Climates Prima, Rolex Movement,
Gold Metal Dial

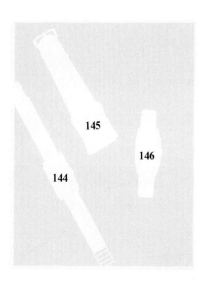

144.
Timeless Elegance ROLEX Ref. No. 41312/3140
Men's Rolex Hinged Case, 1937, 9 ct Yellow Gold,
Case Signed RWC, Rolex 17 Rubies Super Balance Precision Movement,
Metal Dial

145.
Timeless Elegance ROLEX Ref. No. 823867/860
Men's Rolex Hinged Case, 1930, 9 ct Pink Gold,
Case Signed RWC, Rolco 15 Rubies Movement,
Metal Dial

146.
Timeless Elegance ROLEX Ref. No. 838535/2025
Men's Rolex Hinged Case, 1933, 9 ct Yellow Gold,
Case Signed RWC, Rolco 16 Rubies Movement,
Metal Dial

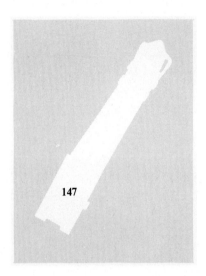

147.
Timeless Elegance ROLEX Ref. No. 28199/1026
Men's Rolex Hinged Case, 1930, 18 ct Two Color White + Yellow Gold,
Case Signed RWC, Rolex Prima 15 Jewels Movement,
Metal Dial

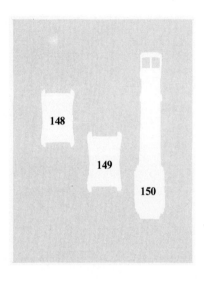

148.
Timeless Elegance ROLEX Ref. No. 64948/971
Men's Rolex Two Piece Prince Case, 1928, 9 ct White + Yellow Gold,
Case Signed RWC LTD, Rolex 15 Rubies 6 Position Observatory Quality #7852 Movement,
Gold Metal Dial

149.
Timeless Elegance ROLEX Ref. No. 30285/1491
Men's Rolex Two Piece Prince Case, 1930, 18 ct White + Yellow Striped Gold,
Case Signed Rolex 25 World's Record's,
18 Jewels Chronometer Rolex Movement,
Two Tone Metal Dial

150.
Timeless Elegance ROLEX Ref. No. 09906/1696
Men's Rolex Two Piece Prince Case, 1931, Steel and Gold,
Case Signed Non Rust Steelium SAR,
15 Jewels Extra Prima Observatory Quality Rolex Movement,
Two Tone Metal Dial

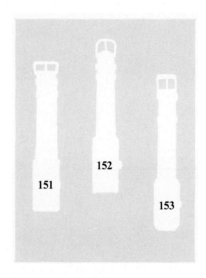

151.
Timeless Elegance ROLEX Ref. No. 983
Men's Rolex Two Piece Case, 1930, 14 ct Pink + Yellow Gold,
Case Signed RWC LTD, 18 Jewels 6 Position Rolex Movement,
White Metal Dial

152.
Timeless Elegance ROLEX Ref. No. 547819/3937
Men's Rolex Two Piece Prince Case, 1942, 14 ct Yellow Gold,
Case Signed Rolex Swiss, 18 Rubies Chronometer Timed 6 Positions Rolex Movement,
Presented to Charles Ridgedale for 25 years service to Eaton, Canada,
Silver Metal Dial

153.
Timeless Elegance ROLEX Ref. No. 42208/1862
Men's Rolex Two Piece Prince Case, 1934, 9 ct Yellow and White Striped Gold,
Case Signed RWC, Rolex 18 Rubies Chronometer Ultra Prima 6 Position #M1410 Movement,
Silver Metal Dial

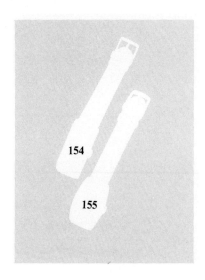

154.
Timeless Elegance ROLEX Ref. No. 47937/1343
Men's Rolex Two Piece Prince Case, 1930, 9 ct Yellow Gold,
Case Signed Rolex S.A., 17 Jewels Extra Prima
6 Position, Observatory Quality Rolex
Movement, Two Tone Metal Dial

155.
Timeless Elegance ROLEX Ref. No. 49261/1287
Men's Rolex Two Piece Case, 1928, 9 ct Yellow Gold,
Case Signed RWC LTD, 17 Jewels, Prima Rolex Movement,
Gold Dial

156.
Timeless Elegance ROLEX Ref. No. 64216/1491
Men's Rolex Two Piece Prince Case, 1935, 18 ct White and Yellow Gold, Digital,
Case Signed RWC LTD, 18 Rubies Chronometer — #3561
6 Position Rolex Movement, White Metal Dial

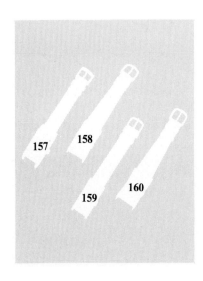

157.
Timeless Elegance ROLEX Ref. No. 604569/3937
Men's Rolex Two Piece Prince Case, 1949, 14 ct Yellow Gold,
Case Signed Rolex, 18 Rubies Chronometer 6 Positions Rolex Movement,
Presented to Elmer Bader to Mark 25 years service to Eaton Canada,
White Metal Dial

158.
Timeless Elegance ROLEX Ref. No. 58093/1490
Men's Rolex Two Piece Prince Case, 1935, 18 ct Pink Gold,
Case Signed RWC LTD, Rolex 17 Jewels
Adjusted 7 Positions Chronometer #2041 Movement,
Two Tone Metal Dial

159.
Timeless Elegance ROLEX Ref. No. 68328/1343A
Rolex Men's Two Piece Prince Case, 1935, 18 ct Yellow Gold,
Case Signed RWC LTD, Rolex 15 Jewels Extra Prima 6 Positions Observatory Quality #72968 Movement,
Engraved Back Geoff Jan 8 1935 HOP.
Yellow Metal Dial

160.
Timeless Elegance ROLEX Ref. No. 309413/1490
Men's Rolex Two Piece Prince Case, 1945, 14 ct Yellow Gold,
Case Signed Rolex 31 Victories,
18 Rubies Chronometer Timed 6 Positions Rolex Movement,
Presented to Edwin E. Jarvis from Eaton Canada
Two Tone Metal Dial

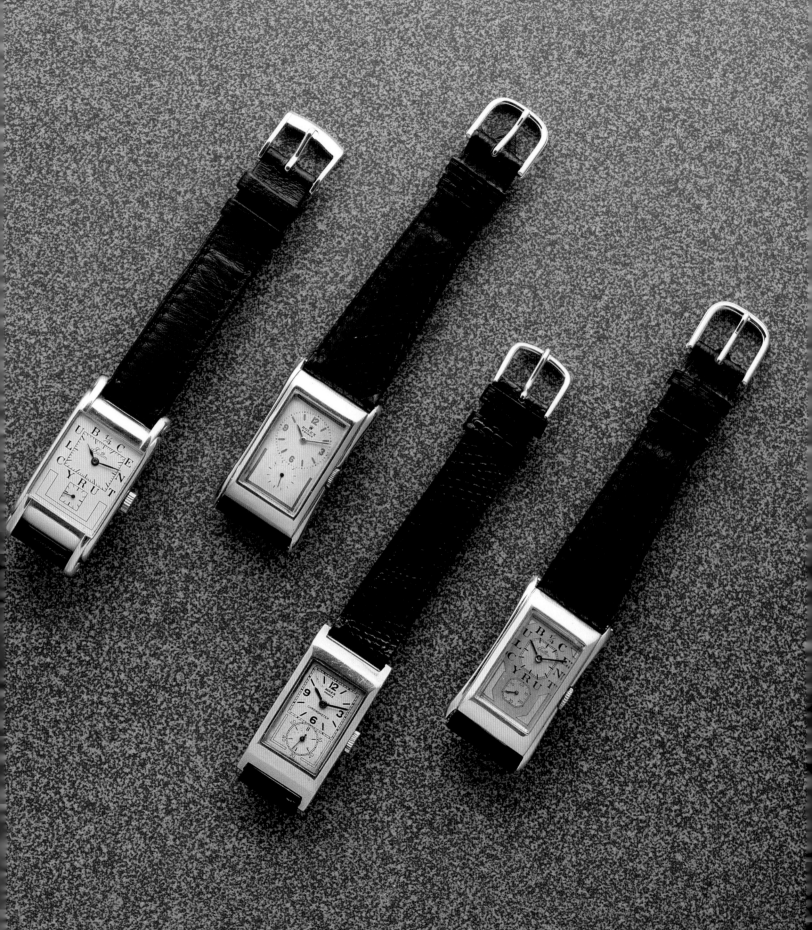

161.
Timeless Elegance ROLEX Ref. No. 74480/971
Men's Rolex Two Piece Prince Case, Sterling Silver, 1929,
15 Rubies, Extra Prima, 6 Positions Observatory Quality,
Two Tone Dial, Flaired Rectangular Case, Movement, Dial,
Case Signed Rolex

162.
Timeless Elegance ROLEX Ref. No. 79461/4684
Men's Rolex 18 ct Pink Gold, 1942,
Subsidiary Seconds Two Piece Case, 17 Jewels, Chronometer,
Case, Dial, Movement Signed Rolex

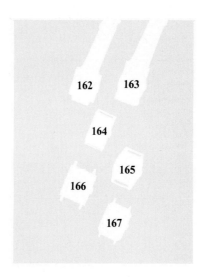

163.
Timeless Elegance ROLEX Ref. No. 764622
Men's Rolex 9 ct Pink Gold, 1932,
Subsidiary Seconds Two Piece Case, 17 Jewels, Prima Movement,
Dial, Case, Movement Signed Rolex

164.
Timeless Elegance ROLEX Ref. No. 021247/188C
Men's Rolex Prince Elegant Steel and Pink Gold Center, 1937,
Two Piece Case, Subsidiary Seconds, 15 Jewels, 25 Records, Dial Signed Cubuchereris,
Case, Dial, Movement Signed Rolex

165.
Timeless Elegance ROLEX Ref. No. 304659
Men's Rolex 9 ct Pink Gold, 1936,
Two Piece Case, Subsidiary Seconds, 17 Jewels Extra Prima Movement,
Case, Dial, Movement Signed Rolex

166.
Timeless Elegance ROLEX Ref. No. 246851/8498/73
Men's Rolex 10 ct Yellow Gold, 1955,
Two Piece Precision Case, Subsidiary Seconds, 18 Rubies 6 Positions, Chronometer,
Case, Dial, Movement Signed Rolex

167.
Timeless Elegance ROLEX Ref. No. 22651/3519
Men's Rolex 18 ct Yellow Gold, 1935,
Hinged Case, 17 Jewels, Subsidiary Seconds, Two Tone Dial,
Case, Dial, Movement Signed Rolex

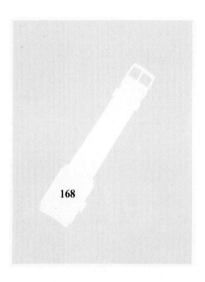

168.
Timeless Elegance ROLEX Ref. No. 256477/1775
Men's Rolex Hinged Case, 1938, Stainless Steel and Lacquer,
Case Signed RWC, 15 Jewels, Hour, Minutes,
Seconds Display.

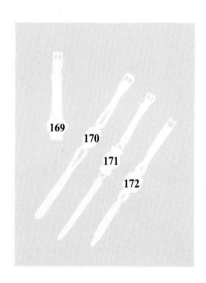

169.
Timeless Elegance ROLEX Ref. No. 47241/3724
Ladies Rolex Oyster Case, 1939, 18 ct Pink Gold,
Subsidiary Seconds, Case Signed Rolex S.A. 31 Victories Geneva-Suisse Haute — Precision,
19 Jewels Rolex Chronometer Auto Rotor Movement,
Metal Dial

170.
Timeless Elegance ROLEX Ref. No. 344778/4211
Ladies Rolex Two Piece Case, 1941, 18 ct Pink Gold,
Case Signed Rolex 31 Victoires De Haute
Precision Geneve Suisse,
Rolex Super Balance 17 Rubies Movement,
Metal Dial

171.
Timeless Elegance ROLEX Ref. No. 23006/2703
Ladies Rolex Three Piece Case, 1936, Steel + Pink Gold,
Subsidiary Seconds, Case Signed Rolex 25 Record's Universels Geneve SAR,
Staybrite, Rolex 15 Rubies Movement, Metal Dial

172.
Timeless Elegance ROLEX Ref. No. 315670/4381
Ladies Rolex Two Piece Case, 1943, 18 ct Pink Gold,
Subsidiary Seconds, Case Signed Rolex 31 Victories Geneve Suisse,
18 Rubies Timed 6 Positions Rolex Movement,
Metal Dial

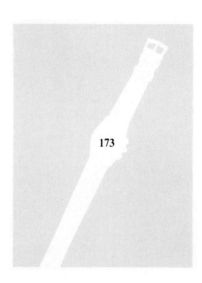

173.
Timeless Elegance ROLEX Ref. No. 57475/3834
Ladies Rolex 18 ct Yellow Gold, 1944, Chronograph
With Register, Auxiliary Seconds and 30 Minutes Register Dial,
Three Piece Case, 17 Jewels, 31 Victoires, Case, Dial, Movement Signed Rolex

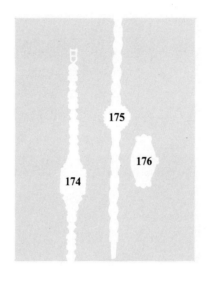

174.
Timeless Elegance ROLEX Ref. No. 94685
Ladies Rolex 18 ct Precision Case, Yellow Gold, 1949,
Two Piece Case, Diamonds and Emeralds, 17 Jewels, 6 Position,
Case, Dial, Movement Signed Rolex

175.
Timeless Elegance ROLEX Ref. No. 119444
Ladies Rolex 18 ct Precision Case, White Gold, 1953, Diamonds,
Two Piece Case, 17 Jewels, 6 Position, Case, Dial, Movement Signed Rolex

176.
Timeless Elegance ROLEX Ref. No. 3127/122
Ladies Rolex 18 ct White Gold with Diamonds, 1926,
Hinged Case, 17 Jewels, Prima Movement,
Case, Dial, Movement Signed Rolex

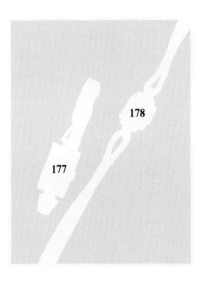

177.
Timeless Elegance ROLEX Ref. No. 68531/1622
Ladies Rolex Two Piece Case, 1938, Stainless Steel,
Case Signed RWC Stay Brite, Rolex 17 Jewels Movement,
Metal Dial

178.
Timeless Elegance ROLEX Ref. No. 346528/4211
Ladies Rolex Two Piece Case, 1948, 18 ct Yellow Gold,
Case Signed Rolex 31 Victoires De Haute Geneve,
17 Jewels Rolex Movement, Metal Dial

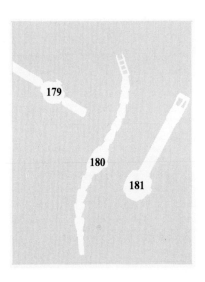

179.
Timeless Elegance ROLEX Ref. No. 307947
Ladies Rolex Two Piece Case, 1941, 9 ct Pink Gold,
Case Signed B&S Made for Rolex, Rolex Precision, 17 Jewels Movement,
Metal Dial

180.
Timeless Elegance ROLEX Ref. No. 172997/T
Ladies Rolex Two Piece Case, 1942, 9 ct Pink Gold,
Case Signed RWC, Tudor 17 Jewels Movement,
Metal Dial

181.
Timeless Elegance ROLEX Ref. No. 34599/015
Ladies Rolex Two Piece Case, 1938, 18 ct White Gold with Diamonds
Case Signed Rolex 7 World Rolex, Rolex Prima
16 Jewels 6 Position for All Climates, White Metal Dial

182.
Timeless Elegance ROLEX Ref. No. 46538/2861
Men's Rolex Oyster Perpetual Case, 1937, 18 ct Pink Gold,
Case Signed Rolex RWC,
Movement Rolex 17 Jewels Prima Timed 6 Positions,
Gold Metal Dial

183.
Timeless Elegance ROLEX Ref. No. 259713/3139
Men's Rolex Oyster Case, 1947, Stainless Steel,
Case Signed Rolex S.A. Geneve-Suisse
31 Victoires, 17 Jewels Super Balance
Rolex Two Positions Movement,
White Metal Dial

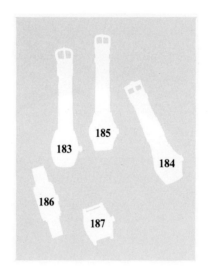

184.
Timeless Elegance ROLEX Ref. No. 145383/6420
Men's Rolex Oyster Case, 1952, Stainless Steel,
Case Signed Rolex, 17 Jewel Rolex Movement,
Black Metal Dial

185.
Timeless Elegance ROLEX Ref. No. 4297112
Men's Rolex Three Piece Case, 1944, Gold Filled,
Case Signed Rolex Keystone Victory,
17 Rubies Super Balance Adjusted
6 Position Observatory Rolex Movement,
Two Tone Metal Dial

186.
Timeless Elegance ROLEX Ref. No. 015757/1880
Men's Rolex Two Piece Case, 1938, Rolesium,
Case Signed Rolex 25 Record's Universals Geneve
SAR, 17 Rubies Ultra Prima Timed
6 Position, Rolex Hairspring Movement,
Silver Metal Dial

187.
Timeless Elegance ROLEX Ref. No. 528014/2940
Men's Rolex Oyster Case, 1940, Stainless Steel,
Case Signed Rolex Geneve Suisse,
19 Jewels Rolex Perpetual, N62861, Chronometer

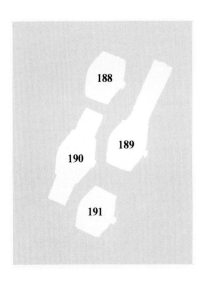

188.
Timeless Elegance ROLEX Ref. No. 726144/6065
Men's Rolex Stainless Steel and Yellow Gold, 1950,
Oyster Perpetual Hooded Case, Center Sweep Seconds Hand,
19 Jewels, Chronometer, Case, Dail, Movement Signed Rolex

189.
Timeless Elegance ROLEX Ref. No. 874200/6065
Men's Rolex Stainless Steel and Yellow Gold, 1952,
Oyster Perpetual Hooded Case, Center Sweep Seconds Hand,
19 Jewels, Chronometer Case, Dial Movement Signed Rolex

190.
Timeless Elegance ROLEX Ref. No. 1V65/5015
Men's Rolex Stainless Steel and Pink Gold, 1948,
Oyster Perpetual Engineturned Hooded Case, Center Sweep Seconds Hand,
19 Jewels, Chronometer, Case, Dial, Movement Signed Rolex

191.
Timeless Elegance ROLEX Ref. No. 943244/6065
Men's Rolex 18 ct Pink Gold, 1949,
Oyster Perpetual Hooded Case, Subidiary Seconds Hand,
19 Jewels, Chronometer, Case, Dial, Movement Signed Rolex

192.
Timeless Elegance ROLEX Ref. No. 381420/3372
Men's Rolex Oyster Perpetual Case, 1944, 18 ct Pink Gold,
Center Sweep Seconds, Case Signed Rolex SAR, Movement 19 Jewels
Rolex Perpetual Chronometer Swiss Made,
Gold Color Metal Dial

193.
Timeless Elegance ROLEX Ref. No. 531312/2764
Men's Rolex Oyster Perpetual Case, 1935, Stainless Steel,
Subsidiary Seconds Hand, Case Signed Rolex Geneve Suisse, 19 Jewels Rolex Perpetual Chronometer,
White Color Metal Dial

194.
Timeless Elegance ROLEX Ref. No. 461533/5050
Men's Rolex Oyster Perpetual Case, 1949, 18 ct Yellow Gold,
Subsidiary Seconds Hand, Case Signed Rolex Geneve Suisse,
19 Jewels Rolex Perpetual Chronometer #70160-85969
Center Sweep Seconds

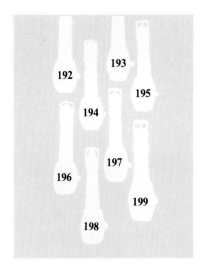

195.
Timeless Elegance ROLEX Ref. No. 452121/3131
Men's Rolex Oyster Perpetual Case, 1950, 9 ct Pink Gold,
Center Sweep Seconds Hand, Case Signed Rolex Perpetual Chronometer,
19 Jewels Rolex Movement #N83905
White Metal Dial

196.
Timeless Elegance ROLEX Ref. No. 548044/3009
Men's Rolex Oyster Perpetual Case, 1946, 9 ct Yellow Gold,
Center Sweep Seconds Hand, Case Signed Rolex RWC LTD,
Movement Certified Precision E8404 18 Rubies Timed 6 Position Chronometer Rolex,
Gold Color Metal Dial

197.
Timeless Elegance ROLEX Ref. No. 381252/2940
Men's Rolex Oyster Perpetual Case, 1942, Stainless Steel + Gold Bezel, Subsidiary Second Hand,
Case Signed Rolex, Movement Rolex Perpetual Chronometer, 19 Jewels,
White Metal Dial

198.
Timeless Elegance ROLEX Ref. No. 58346
Men's Rolex Oyster Perpetual Case, 1935 Stainless Steel,
Subsidiary Second Hand, Case Signed Oyster Watch Co.
Movement Signed Rolex Perpetual Chronometer, 19 Jewels,
White Metal Dial

199.
Timeless Elegance ROLEX Ref. No. 714425/6075
Men's Rolex Oyster Perpetual Case, 1949, 18 ct Yellow Gold, with Date, Center Sweep Seconds,
Case Signed Rolex RWC, Movement G19314-36019 19 Jewels,
Gold Metal Dial with Date

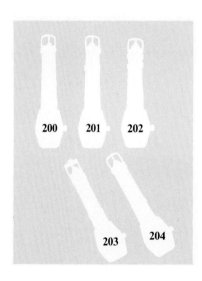

200.
Timeless Elegance ROLEX Ref. No. 151018/2764
Men's Rolex Oyster Perpetual Case, 1935, Stainless Steel, Subsidiary Second Hand,
Case Signed Oyster Watch Co Geneve-Swiss Brevetee-SAR,
Movement 19 Jewels #17226 Rolex Perpetual,
Gold Metal Dial

201.
Timeless Elegance ROLEX Ref. No. 661575/5050
Men's Rolex Oyster Perpetual Case 1949, Stainless Steel,
Center Sweep Seconds Hand, Case Signed Rolex SAR,
Rolex 19 Jewels Perpetual Movement #21057-N8439,
White Metal Dial

202.
Timeless Elegance ROLEX Ref. No. 221069/2765
Men's Rolex Oyster Perpetual Case, 1935, Stainless Steel,
Case Signed Brevetee Rolex SA Geneve Swisse 31 Victoires Haute Precision RWC LTD,
Movement Ultra Prima Chronometer Timed 6 Positions 18 Rubies,
White Metal Dial

203.
Timeless Elegance ROLEX Ref. No. 628719/5015
Men's Rolex Oyster Perpetual Case, 1949, 9 ct Pink Gold, Center Sweep Second Hand,
Case Signed RWC LTD, 19 Jewel Rolex Oyster Chronometer,
Gold Metal Dial

204.
Timeless Elegance ROLEX Ref. No. 660273/5011
Men's Rolex Oyster Perpetual Case, 1949, 9 ct Gold Top Stainless Steel, Center Sweep Second Hand,
Case Signed Rolex, Movement 49468-N96518 Rolex 19 Jewels,
Gold Metal Dial

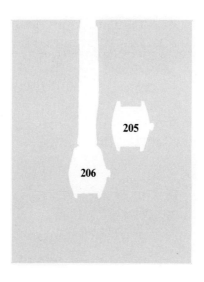

205.
Timeless Elegance ROLEX Ref. No. 746135/5050
Men's Rolex Stainless Steel Oyster Perpetual, 1950,
Center Sweep Seconds Hand, Chronometer,
19 Jewels #N9216/22541, Case, Dail, Movement Signed Rolex

206.
Timeless Elegance ROLEX Ref. No. 225611/1858
Rolex 18 ct Pink Gold, Oyster Perpetual, 1931,
Center sweep Seconds Hand, 24 Hour Dial, Mercedes Hands,
19 Jewels, Chronometer, Case, Dial, Movement Signed Rolex

207.
Timeless Elegance ROLEX Ref. No. 96271/2764
Men's Rolex Stainless Steel Oyster Perpetual, 1936,
Subsidiary Seconds Hand, 19 Jewels Chronometer, Case,
Dial, Movement Signed Rolex

208.
Timeless Elegance ROLEX Ref. No. 289835/3133
Men's Rolex 10 ct Gold Top Stainless Steel Black, 1950,
Oyster Perpetual, Subsidiary Seconds Hands, 19 Jewels Chronometer, Dial,
and Movement Signed Rolex, Case Signed RWC.

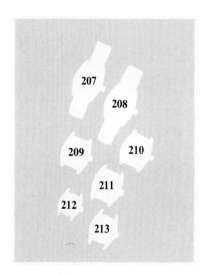

209.
Timeless Elegance ROLEX Ref. No. 605461/5015
Men's Rolex 18 ct Yellow Gold, 1948,
Oyster Perpetual, Center Sweep Second Hand,
19 Jewels Chronometer, Dial, Case, Movement Signed Rolex

210.
Timeless Elegance ROLEX Ref. No. 742612/3134
Men's Rolex Stainless Steel and Gold Bezel, 1942,
Oyster Perpetual, Center Sweep Seconds Hand,
19 Jewels Chronometer, Dial, Case, Movement Signed Rolex

211.
Timeless Elegance ROLEX Ref. No. 894622/2764
Men's Rolex 18 ct Pink Gold, 1936,
Oyster Perpetual, Center Sweep Seconds Hand, 19 Jewels Chronometer,
Case, Dial, Movement Signed Rolex

212.
Timeless Elegance ROLEX Ref. No. 741225/6006
Ladies Rolex 18 ct Pink Gold, 1954,
Oyster Perpetual, Subsidiary Seconds Hand, Black Dial,
19 Jewels Chronometer, Case, Dial, Movement Signed Rolex

213.
Timeless Elegance ROLEX Ref. No. 842103/6006
Men's Rolex 18 ct Yellow Gold, 1953,
Oyster Perpetual, Center Sweep Seconds Hands
19 Jewels Chronometer, Case, Dial, Movement Signed Rolex

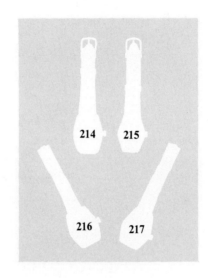

214.
Timeless Elegance ROLEX Ref. No. 634815/5011
Men's Rolex Oyster Perpetual Case, 1940, 10 ct Yellow Gold, Center Sweep Second Hand,
Case Signed RWC LTD, Rolex 19 Jewels Perpetual #93112-54824 Movement,
White Metal Dial

215.
Timeless Elegance ROLEX Ref. No. 582461/6006
Men's Rolex Oyster Perpetual Case, 1950, 10 ct Yellow Gold,
Center Sweep Second Hand, Case Signed Rolex, 19 Jewels Super Precsion Movement #14495,
Black Metal Dial

216.
Timeless Elegance ROLEX Ref. No. 492673/3131
Men's Rolex Oyster Perpetual Case, 1950, 18 ct Pink Gold,
Center Sweep Second Hand, Case Signed Rolex Perpetual Chronometer,
19 Jewels Automatic Rolex Movement,
White Metal Dial

217.
Timeless Elegance ROLEX Ref. No. 532411/5050
Men's Rolex Oyster Perpetual Case 1948, 9 ct Pink Gold, Center Sweep Second Hand,
Case Signed RWC LTD, Rolex Perpetual Chronometer 19 Jewels Movement,
Gold Metal Dial

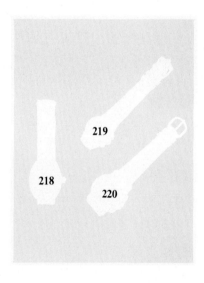

218.
Timeless Elegance ROLEX Ref. No. 65377
Men's Rolex 18 ct Yellow Gold, 1929,
One Button Chronograph with Thirty Minutes Register Dial,
Two Piece Case, 19 Jewels Lever Escapement, Case, Movement and Dial Signed Rolex

219.
Timeless Elegance ROLEX Ref. No. 57475/3834
Ladies Rolex 18 ct Yellow Gold, 1946,
Three Piece Case, Small Square Button, Chronograph,
30 Minutes Register Dial, 17 Jewels,
Lever Escapement, Case, Movement and Dial Signed Rolex

220.
Timeless Elegance ROLEX Ref. No. 354184/3319
Men's Rolex 18 ct Yellow Gold, 1939,
Square Buttons Chronograph with Enamel Dial with 30 Minutes Register,
Three Piece Case, 17 Jewels Lever Escapement, Case, Movement and Dial Signed Rolex

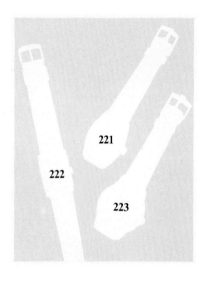

221.
Timeless Elegance ROLEX Ref. No. 74623/6065
Men's Rolex Oyster Case, 1940, Steel and Yellow Gold, Center Sweep Seconds Hand,
Case Signed Rolex Geneve, Rolex 19 Jewels Chronometer Perpetual,
White Metal Dial

222.
Timeless Elegance ROLEX Ref. No. 46632/3260
Men's Rolex Two Piece Case, 1942, 9 ct Pink Gold, Asymmetrical,
Subsidiary Seconds Hand, Case Signed Rolex 31 Records Universals Geneve-Suisse.
Rolex Standard Quality
15 Rubies Swiss Made, White Metal Dial

223.
Timeless Elegance ROLEX Ref. No. 213/8171
Men's Rolex Three Piece Case, 1955, Steel and Pink Gold
Subsidiary Seconds Hand, Case Signed Rolex Geneve-Suisse,
17 Jewels Rolex Perpetual Chronometer Super Balance,
Day-Date-Month-Moonphase, White Metal Dial

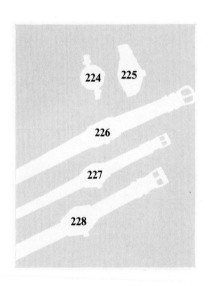

224.
Timeless Elegance ROLEX Ref. No. 039092/3472
Ladies Rolex Two Piece Case, 1936, Stainless Steel,
Case Signed Rolex S.A., 15 Rubies Standard Quality
Elinvar Hairspring Rolex Movement,
White Metal Dial

225.
Timeless Elegance ROLEX Ref. No. 103870/6505
Ladies Rolex Oyster Case, 1953, Steel and Yellow Gold, Subsidiary Seconds Hand,
Case Signed Rolex S.A., 17 Jewels Rolex Perpetual Movement,
White Metal Dial

226.
Timeless Elegance ROLEX Ref. No. 79/8126
Ladies Rolex Two Piece Oyster Case, 1950, 18 ct Yellow Gold,
Subsidiary Seconds Hand, Case Signed Rolex Swiss, 19 Jewels Rolex Perpetual,
Black Metal Dial

227.
Timeless Elegance ROLEX Ref. No. 53042/3869
Ladies Rolex Oyster Case, 1941, 18 ct Pink Gold, Subsidiary Seconds Hand,
Case Signed Rolex, 19 Jewels Rolex Perpetual Movement,
White Metal Dial

228.
Timeless Elegance ROLEX Ref. No. 38296/2595
Men's Rolex Oyster Case, 1938, 9 ct Yellow Gold,
Subsidiary Second Hand, Case Signed RWC LTD, 17 Jewels Rolex Movement,
White Metal Dial

229.
Timeless Elegance ROLEX Ref. No. M016059/91577
Men's Rolex 9 ct Pink Gold, Square Case, 1946, Chronometer, Auxiliary Seconds,
18 Rubies, Timed 6 Positions, Super Balance, #E20410, Movement, Case, Dial Signed Rolex

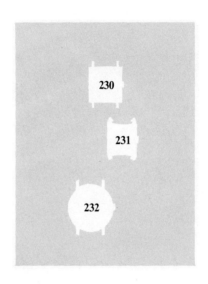

230.
Timeless Elegance ROLEX Ref. No. 82615/9092
Men's Rolex 18 ct Pink Gold, 1957, Two Piece Case, 17 Jewels 6 Position,
Movement, Case, Dial Signed Rolex

231.
Timeless Elegance ROLEX Ref. No. 52841/3790
Men's Rolex 18 ct Pink Gold, 1943, Precision,
Two Piece Case, 17 Jewels For All Climate, 6 Position,
Case, Dial, Movement Signed Rolex

232.
Timeless Elegance ROLEX Ref. No. 36128/4410
Men's Rolex 18 ct Pink Gold, Precision, 1945,
Two Piece Case, 17 Jewel 6 Position, Chronometer, Subsidiary Seconds,
Case, Dial, Movement Signed Rolex

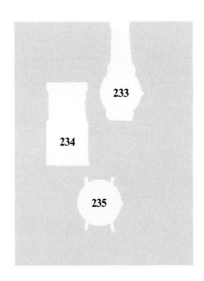

233.
Timeless Elegance ROLEX Ref. No. 68421/4579
Men's Rolex Precision 18 ct Pink Gold, Round, 1950, Center Sweep Seconds Hand,
Super Balance, Officially Certified Chronometer,
Rolex-17 Jewels #E75476 Movement, Case, Dial Signed Rolex

234.
Timeless Elegance ROLEX Ref. No. 4751/996
Rolex Folding Travel Watch, Sterling Silver and Enamel, 1928,
Subsidiary Seconds Hand, 17 Jewels, Four Piece Case, Movement, Dial, Case Signed Rolex

235.
Timeless Elegance ROLEX Ref. No. 374345/4399
Men's Rolex Precision 14 ct Top, Stainless Steel Back, Round Case, 1948,
Auxiliar Seconds Super Balance, 17 Jewels Chronometer, Movement, Case, Dial Signed Rolex

236.
Timeless Elegance ROLEX Ref. No. 400000/3853
Men's Rolex 18 ct Pink Gold, 1947, Chronograph with Square Buttons,
Auxiliary Seconds and 30 Minutes Register,
17 Jewels Lever Escapement Super balance,
Self-Compensating Breguet Balance Spring,
Case Dial Movement Signed Rolex

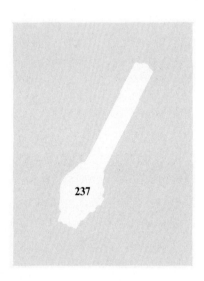

237.
Timeless Elegance ROLEX Ref. No. 47825/3780
Men's Rolex Chronograph Oyster Case, 1943, 18 ct Pink Gold, Square Buttons,
Minute and Hour Register, Case Signed Rolex S.A., 17 Jewels Rolex Movement,
Gold Metal Dial

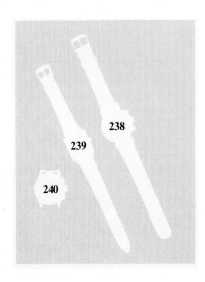

238.
Timeless Elegance ROLEX Ref. No. 481020/6529
Men's Rolex Chronograph Three Piece Case, 1942, Stainless Steel, Square Buttons,
with Register, Case Signed Rolex Geneve, 17 Jewels Rolex Movement,
White Metal Dial

239.
Timeless Elegance ROLEX Ref. No. 456421/4470
Men's Rolex Square Two Piece Case, 1947, 14 ct Yellow Gold,
Case Signed Rolex S.A.,
17 Jewels Super Balance Chronometer Rolex Movement #33900,
Black Metal Dial

240.
Timeless Elegance ROLEX Ref. No. 030482/2508
Men's Rolex Chronograph Three Piece Case, 1939, Stainless Steel,
Case Signed Rolex 31 Victoires, 17 Jewels Rolex Movement,
Black Metal Dial

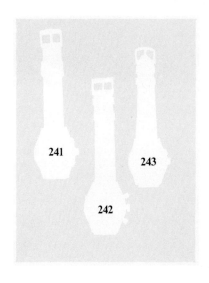

241.
Timeless Elegance ROLEX Ref. No. 402223/3827
Men's Rolex Stainless Steel Chronograph, 1946,
With Square Buttons, Auxiliary Seconds and 30 Minutes Register,
17 Jewels Copper Dial, Movement, Case and Dial Signed Rolex

242.
Timeless Elegance ROLEX Ref. No. 847024/6036
Men's Rolex Stainless Steel Round Buttons Chronograph, 1956, Oyster Case,
Water proof with Day, Date, Month Indicated,
12 Hours and 30 Minutes Registers, 17 Jewels, Case, Dial, Movement Signed Rolex

243.
Timeless Elegance ROLEX Ref. No. 402521/3695
Men's Rolex Stainless Steel Chronograph, 1947,
With Square Buttons, Register, Tachometer and Telemeter
Auxiliary Seconds and 30 Minutes. Register, Two Tone Silver Dial,
17 Jewels, Copper Dial, Case, Dial and Movement Signed Rolex

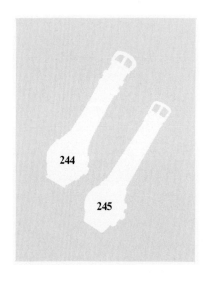

244.
Timeless Elegance ROLEX Ref. No. 931356/81806
Men's Rolex 18K Yellow Gold, 1952 Chronograph
With Square Buttons, Register, Triple Date and Moon Phase,
Auxiliary Seconds and 30 Minutes Register Dials,
Aperture for the Days of the Week, the Months and the Moon,
17 Jewels, Case, Dial, Movement Signed Rolex

245.
Timeless Elegance ROLEX Ref. No. 269674/81806
Men's Rolex 18K Pink Gold 1950, Chronograph,
With Square Buttons, Register, Triple Date and Moon Phase,
Auxiliary Seconds and 30 Minutes Registered Dials,
Aperture for the Days of the Week, the Months and the Moon,
17 Jewels, Case, Dial, Movement Signed Rolex

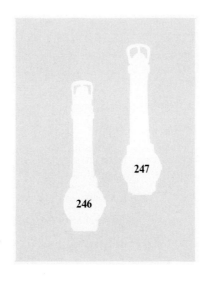

246.
Timeless Elegance ROLEX Ref. No. 647251/8144
Men's Rolex 18K Pink Gold, 1956, Center Sweep Seconds Hand, Round Case,
Flattened Lugs, Two Piece Case, 17 Jewels, Super Balnce Officially Certified Chronometer #E68724
7 Position, Movement, Case, Dial Signed Rolex

247.
Timeless Elegance ROLEX Ref. No. 67546/4579
Men's Rolex 9 ct, Pink Gold 1949, Round Case Center Sweep Seconds Hand,
Super Balance, Officially Certified Chronometer,
17 Jewels #E71843 Movement, Case, Dial Signed Rolex

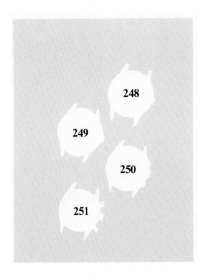

248.
Timeless Elegance ROLEX Ref. No. 341/8171
Men's Rolex Stainless Steel, 1960, Moon Phase
Day, Date, Month, Perpetual, Two Piece Case, Automatic,
18 Jewel Super Balance, Case, Dial, Movement Signed Rolex

249.
Timeless Elegance ROLEX Ref. No. 625/8171
Men's Rolex 18 ct Pink Gold, 1960,
18 Jewels, Day, Date, Month, Perpetual,
18 Jewel, Two Piece Case, Super Balance, Case Dial Movement Signed Rolex

250.
Timeless Elegance ROLEX Ref. No. 721681/3827
Men's Rolex 18 ct Pink Gold, 1945,
Chronograph With Square Buttons, Register and
Tachometer Auxiliary Dials for the Seconds and 12 Hours and 30 Minutes.
17 Jewels Lever Escapement, Case, Dial, Movement Signed Rolex

251.
Timeless Elegance ROLEX Ref. No. 7481/6054
Men's Rolex 18 ct Pink Gold, 1942, Water Proof
Chronograph With Round Buttons Register and Tachometer,
Auxiliary Dials for the Seconds and 12 Hours and 30 Minutes
17 Jewels Lever Escapement
Case, Dial, Movement Signed Rolex

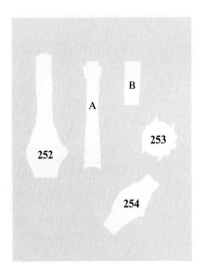

252.
Timeless Elegance ROLEX Ref. No. 59293160/166
Men's Rolex Stainless Steel, 1987,
Oyster Perpetual Sea Dweller. Case, Dial, Movement Signed Rolex

253.
Timeless Elegance ROLEX Ref. No. 685219/3525
Men's Rolex Stainless Steel, 1945,
Oyster Two Piece Case, Chronograph, 17 Jewels, With Minute Register,
Case, Dial, Movement Signed Rolex

254.
Timeless Elegance ROLEX Ref. No. 616282/2764
Men's Rolex 18 ct, Yellow Gold, 1936,
Oyster Perpetual Chronometer 19 Jewels Case, Dial, Movement Signed

A.
Rolex Stainless Steel and Pink Gold Bracelet for the Bubble Back 1945

B.
Rolex 9 ct Pink Gold Buckle with Steel Folding Section 1945

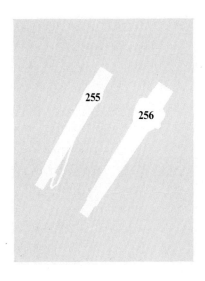

255.
Timeless Elegance ROLEX Ref. No. 1461992/G189
Ladies Rolex Two Piece Case, 1960, 18 ct White Gold with Diamonds,
Case Signed Rolex S.B. Geneve, 17 Jewels Rolex Pression Movement,
Silver Metal Dial

256.
Timeless Elegance ROLEX Ref. No. 125488/3151
Ladies Rolex Two Piece Case, 1963, 18K Yellow Gold,
Case Signed Rolex S.A. Geneve, 18 Rubies Rolex Movement #1400,
White Metal Dial

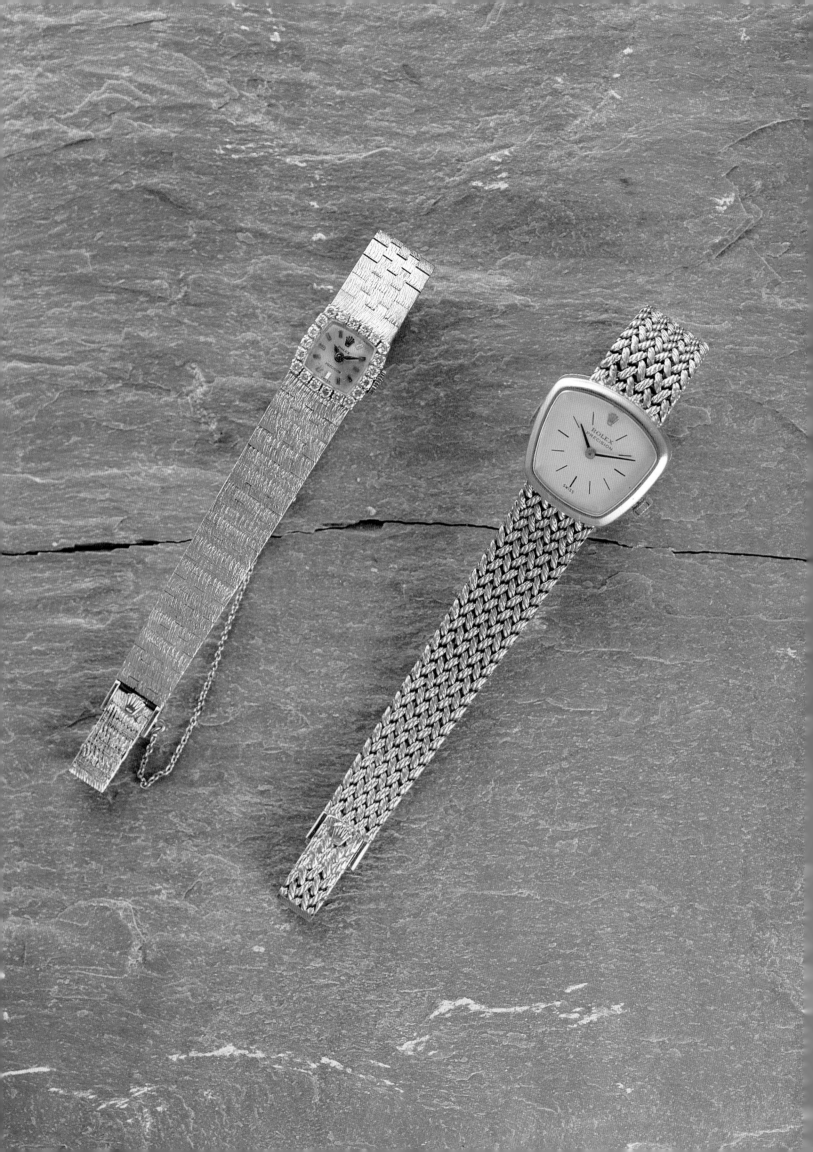

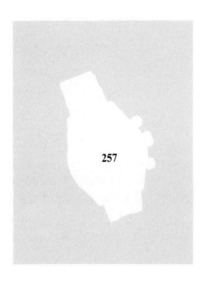

257.
Timeless Elegance ROLEX Ref. No. 4089949/6263
Men's Rolex Chronograph Oyster Case, 1962, 14 ct Yellow Gold Case Signed Rolex Geneve,
17 Jewels Lever Escapement Rolex Movement,
Black Metal Dial

REFERENCES

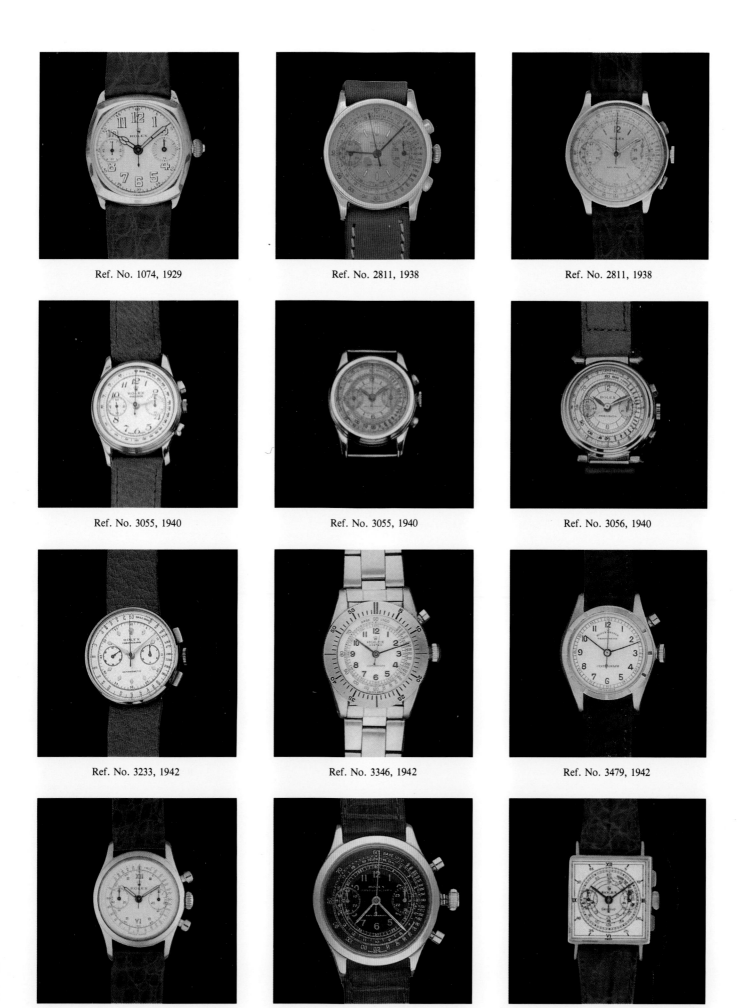

Ref. No. 1074, 1929

Ref. No. 2811, 1938

Ref. No. 2811, 1938

Ref. No. 3055, 1940

Ref. No. 3055, 1940

Ref. No. 3056, 1940

Ref. No. 3233, 1942

Ref. No. 3346, 1942

Ref. No. 3479, 1942

Ref. No. 3481, 1944

Ref. No. 3525, 1944

Ref. No. 3529, 1944

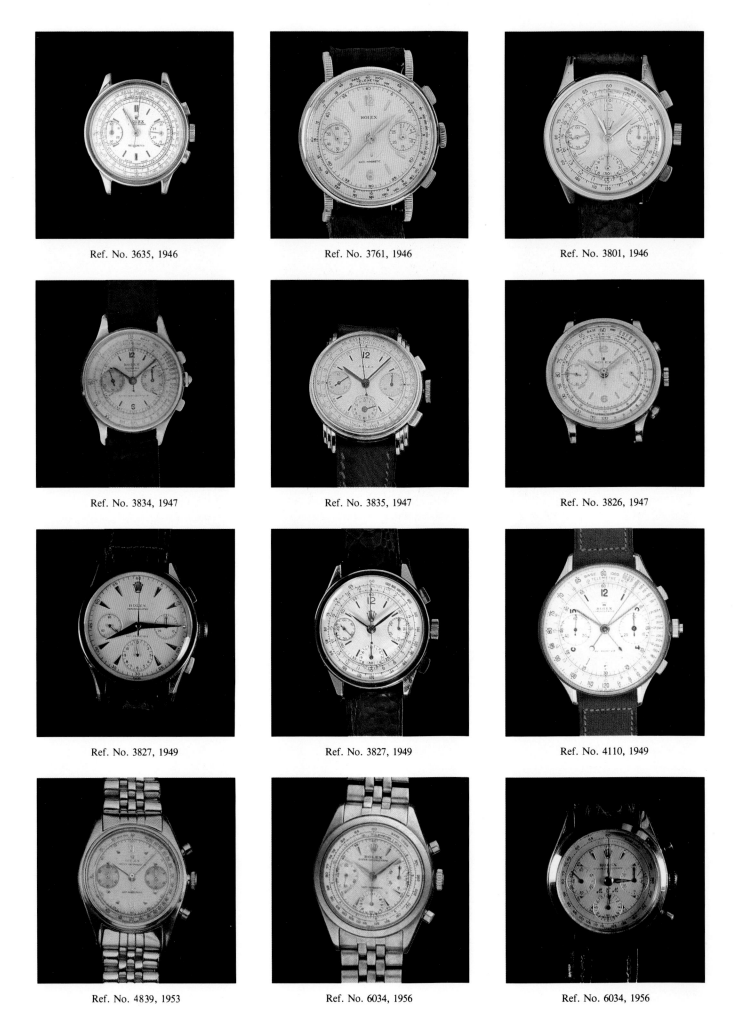

Ref. No. 3635, 1946

Ref. No. 3761, 1946

Ref. No. 3801, 1946

Ref. No. 3834, 1947

Ref. No. 3835, 1947

Ref. No. 3826, 1947

Ref. No. 3827, 1949

Ref. No. 3827, 1949

Ref. No. 4110, 1949

Ref. No. 4839, 1953

Ref. No. 6034, 1956

Ref. No. 6034, 1956

Ref. No. 6034, 1957

Ref. No. 6034, 1957

Ref. No. 6054, 1957

Ref. No. 6238, 1960

Ref. No. 6238, 1960

Ref. No. 6238, 1970

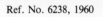

Ref. No. 6238, 1970

Ref. No. 6263, 1970

Ref. No. 6263, 1970

Ref. No. 8171, 1960

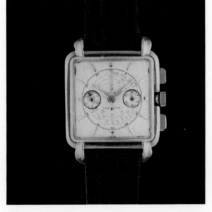

Ref. No. 8206, 1953

Ref. No. 8206, 1955

Ref. No. 971, 1928

Ref. No. 971, 1929

Ref. No. 971, 1929

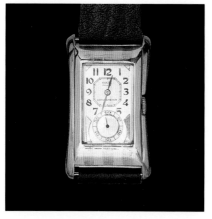

Ref. No. 971, 1930

Ref. No. 971, 1930

Ref. No. 971, 1930

Ref. No. 971, 1930

Ref. No. 971, 1930

Ref. No. 971, 1930

Ref. No. 971, 1930

Ref. No. 971, 1931

Ref. No. 971, 1931

Ref. No. 971, 1931

Ref. No. 971, 1932

Ref. No. 971, 1932

Ref. No. 971, 1933

Ref. No. 971, 1933

Ref. No. 971, 1938

Ref. No. 1343, 1935

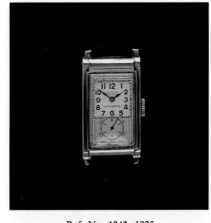

Ref. No. 1343, 1935

Ref. No. 1343, 1935

Ref. No. 1490, 1928

Ref. No. 1490, 1928

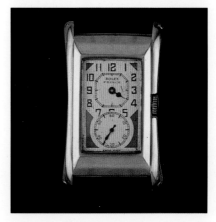

Ref. No. 1490, 1928

Ref. No. 1490, 1931

Ref. No. 1490, 1932

Ref. No. 1490, 1933

Ref. No. 1490, 1933

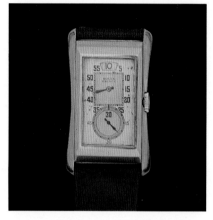

Ref. No. 1491, 1931

Ref. No. 1491, 1931

Ref. No. 2246, 1936

Ref. No. 2245, 1936

Ref. No. 2246, 1936

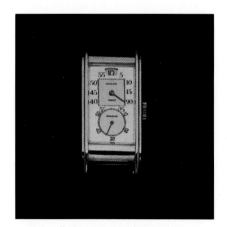

Ref. No. 2246, 1936

Ref. No. 2247, 1936

Ref. No. 2540, 1937

Ref. No. 2540, 1937

Ref. No. 2540, 1937

Ref. No. 2540, 1937

Ref. No. 2541, 1937

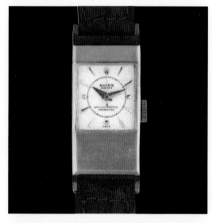

Ref. No. 3361, 1937

Ref. No. 3361, 1937

Ref. No. 3362, 1939

Ref. No. 3362, 1939

Ref. No. 3937, 1945

Ref. No. 3937, 1945

Ref. No. 3937, 1945

Ref. No. 3937, 1945

263

Ref. No. 4767, 1949

Ref. No. 4768, 1947

Ref. No. 6036, 1949

Ref. No. 6036, 1951

Ref. No. 6036, 1951

Ref. No. 6036, 1951

Ref. No. 6062, 1953

Ref. No. 6062, 1949

Ref. No. 6062, 1949

Ref. No. 6062, 1953

Ref. No. 6062, 1953

Ref. No. 6062, 1953

Ref. No. 6062, 1955

Ref. No. 6062, 1953

Ref. No. 8124, 1955

Ref. No. 8171, 1959

Ref. No. 81806, 1951

Ref. No. 547, 1920

Ref. No. 801, 1928

Ref. No. 868, 1928

Ref. No. 912, 1930

Ref. No. 1822, 1933

Ref. No. 2869, 1933

Ref. No. 3028, 1937

Ref. No. 3029, 1937

Ref. No. 3065, 1938

Ref. No. 3065, 1938

Ref. No. 3188, 1938

Ref. No. 3536, 1946

Ref. No. 3536, 1946

Ref. No. 3950, 1948

Ref. No. 6085, 1951

Ref. No. 6808, 1985

French Case, 1938

Military Case, 1943

Military Case, 1943

ROLEX OYSTER CASE PRODUCTION DATES

by Serial Number

Serial #	Date	Serial #	Date	Serial #	Date
28,000	1926	543,400	1948	2,689,700	1969
30,430	1927	608,500	1949	2,952,600	1970
32,960	1928	673,600	1950	3,215,500	1971
35,390	1929	738,700	1951	3,478,400	1972
37,820	1930	803,800	1952	3,741,300	1973
40,250	1931	868,900	1953	4,004,200	1974
42,680	1932	934,000	1954	4,267,100	1975
45,000	1934	1,012,000	1955	4,539,000	1976
63,000	1935	1,090,000	1956	5,006,000	1977
81,000	1936	1,168,000	1957	5,482,000	1978
99,000	1937	1,246,000	1958	5,958,000	1979
117,000	1938	1,324,000	1959	6,434,000	1980
135,000	1939	1,402,000	1960	6,910,000	1981
164,600	1940	1,480,000	1961	7,386,000	1982
194,200	1941	1,558,000	1962	7,862,000	1983
223,800	1942	1,636,000	1963	8,338,000	1984
253,400	1943	1,714,000	1964	8,814,000	1985
283,000	1944	1,792,000	1965	9,290,000	1986
348,100	1945	1,871,000	1966	9,766,000	1987
413,200	1946	2,163,900	1967	9,999,999	1987 1/2
478,300	1947	2,426,800	1968	R,000,000	1987 1/2

Note: The above Rolex Oyster case serial number list is as accurate as our current information will allow. We have not verified that when Non Oyster watches such as Chronographs, Dress and Cellini case serial numbers when used with this chart may not give you the correct date.

This page was supplied by the Vintage American and European Wrist Watch Price Guide by Roy Ehrhardt & Ken Specht.

TIMELESS ELEGANCE

LATEST MODELS FROM ROLEX

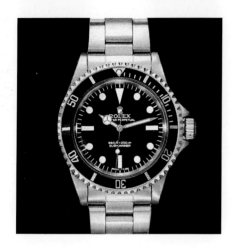  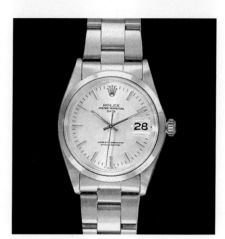

Ref. 1002/0
OYSTER PERPETUAL,
chronometer in steel.
Oyster bracelet.
Waterproof to 100 m/330 feet.
Selfwinding.

Ref. 1005/3
OYSTER PERPETUAL,
chronometer in
steel and gold.
Oyster bracelet.
Waterproof to 100 m/330 feet.
Selfwinding.

Ref. 1016/0
Oyster Perpetual,
EXPLORER I,
chronometer in steel.
Oyster bracelet.
Waterproof to 100 m/330 feet.
Selfwinding.

Ref. 5513
Oyster Perpetual
SUBMARINER, chronometer in steel.
Fliplock bracelet.
Graduated revolving bezel for
observation of decompression times.
Special Oyster case with shoulders
protecting the Triplock winding crown,
waterproof to 200 m/660 feet.
Selfwinding.
Sapphire crystal.

Ref. 6694/0
OYSTERDATE in steel.
Oyster bracelet.
Waterproof to 100 m/330 feet.
Calendar.
Manual winding.

Ref. 15000
Oyster Perpetual DATE,
chronometer in steel.
Oyster bracelet.
Waterproof to 100 m/330 feet.
Selfwinding.

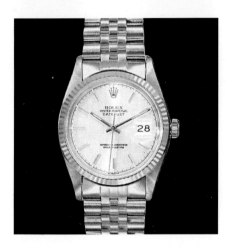  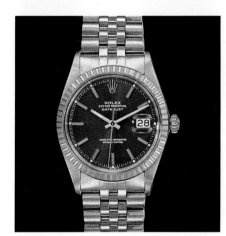

Ref. 15010
Oyster Perpetual DATE,
chronometer in steel.
Oyster bracelet.
Waterproof to 100 m/330 feet.
Selfwinding.

Ref. 15053
Oyster Perpetual DATE
chronometer in steel and gold.
Oyster bracelet.
Waterproof to 100 m/330 feet.
Selfwinding.

Ref. 16000
Oyster Perpetual
DATEJUST, chronometer in steel.
Jubilee bracelet.
Waterproof to 100 m/330 feet.
Selfwinding.

Ref. 16013
Oyster Perpetual
DATEJUST,
chronometer in steel and gold.
Jubilee bracelet.
Waterproof to 100 m/330 feet.
Selfwinding.

Ref. 16014
Oyster Perpetual
DATEJUST, chronometer
in steel with white gold bezel.
Steel Jubilee bracelet.
Waterproof to 100 m/330 feet.
Selfwinding.

Ref. 16030
Oyster Perpetual
DATEJUST,
chronometer in steel.
Jubilee bracelet.
Waterproof to 100 m/330 feet.
Selfwinding.

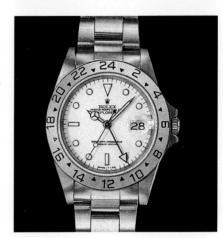

Ref. 16078
Oyster Perpetual
DATEJUST, chronometer in 18 ct gold
with "bark" finish.
Matching Jubilee bracelet.
Waterproof to 100 m/330 feet.
Selfwinding.
Sapphire crystal.

Ref. 16253
Oyster Perpetual
DATEJUST, chronometer in steel and gold.
Jubilee bracelet.
Revolving bezel for easy
measuring of time spans
(long distance calls, parking meters etc.).
Waterproof to 100 m/330 feet.
Selfwinding.

Ref. 16520
Oyster Perpetual
COSMOGRAPH, chronometer in steel.
Oyster bracelet.
Screw-down push-buttons and Triplock
winding crown.
Engraved bezel calibrated for immediate
read-off of hourly speeds, production rates etc.
Waterproof to 100 m/330 feet.
Selfwinding. Sapphire crystal.

Ref. 16523
Oyster Perpetual
COSMOGRAPH,
chronometer in steel and gold.
Oyster bracelet.
Screw-down push-buttons and Triplock
winding crown.
Engraved bezel
calibrated for immediate read-off
of hourly speeds,
production rates etc.
Waterproof to 100 m/330 feet.
Selfwinding.
Sapphire crystal.

Ref. 16528
Oyster Perpetual
COSMOGRAPH,
chronometer in 18 ct gold.
Oyster bracelet.
Screw-down push-buttons
and Triplock winding crown.
Engraved bezel
calibrated for immediate read-off
of hourly speeds,
production rates etc.
Waterproof to 100 m/330 feet.
Selfwinding.
Sapphire crystal.

Ref. 16550
Oyster Perpetual,
EXPLORER II,
chronometer in steel.
Oyster bracelet.
24-hour bezel and hand
and independently adjustable 12-hour
hand allow simultaneous use
for a second time-zone.
Case with shoudlers protecting
the winding crown.
Waterproof to 100 m/330 feet.
Selfwinding.
Sapphire crystal.

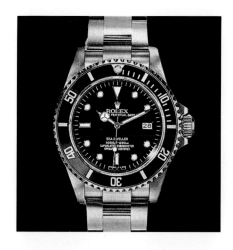  

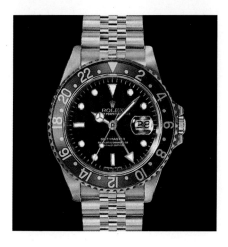 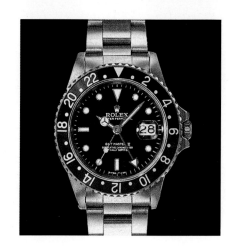 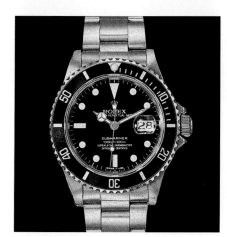

Ref. 16660
Oyster Perpetual Date
SEA-DWELLER 4000,
chronometer in steel.
Fliplock bracelet.
Graduated revolving bezel for
observation of decompression times.
Special Oyster case with gas escape
valve for saturation diving, shoulders
protecting the Triplock winding crown.
Waterproof to 1,220 m/4,000 feet.
Selfwinding. Sapphire crystal.

Ref. 16750
Oyster Perpetual
GMT-MASTER,
chronometer in steel.
Oyster bracelet.
Revolving 24-hour bezel
and hand allow simultaneous
use for a second time-zone.
Case with shoulders protecting
the winding crown,
waterproof to 100 m/330 feet.
Selfwinding.

Ref. 16753
Oyster Perpetual
GMT-MASTER, chronometer
in steel and gold.
Jubilee bracelet.
Revolving 24-hour bezel
and hand allow simultaneous
use for a second time-zone.
Case with shoulders protecting the winding
crown,
waterproof to 100 m/330 feet.
Selfwinding.

Ref. 16758
Oyster Perpetual
GMT-MASTER,
chronometer in 18 ct gold.
Jubilee bracelet.
Revolving 24-hour bezel
and hand allow simultaneous
use for a second time-zone.
Case with shoulders protecting
the winding crown,
waterproof to 100 m/330 feet.
Selfwinding.
Sapphire crystal.

Ref. 16760
Oyster Perpetual
GMT-MASTER II, chronometer
in steel. Oyster bracelet.
Revolving 24-hour bezel and hand
and the independently adjustable
12-hour hand allow
simultaneous use for any two time-zones.
Case with shoulders protecting
the winding crown,
waterproof to 100 m/330 feet.
Selfwinding.
Sapphire crystal.

Ref. 16800
Oyster Perpetual Date
SUBMARINER,
chronometer in steel.
Fliplock bracelet.
Graduated revolving bezel for
observation of decompression times.
Special Oyster case with shoulders
protecting the Triplock winding crown,
waterproof to 300 m/1,000 feet.
Selfwinding.
Sapphire crystal.

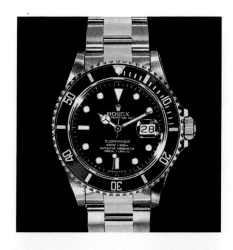

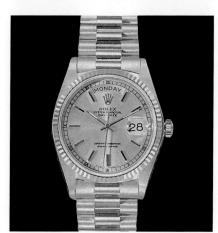

Ref. 16803
Oyster Perpetual Date,
SUBMARINER, chronometer
in steel and gold.
Fliplock bracelet.
Graduated revolving bezel for observation
of decompression times.
Special Oyster case with shoulders
protecting the Triplock winding crown,
waterproof to 300 m/1,000 feet.
Selfwinding.
Sapphire crystal.

Ref. 16808
Oyster Perpetual Date
SUBMARINER,
chronometer in 18 ct gold.
Fliplock bracelet.
Graduated revolving bezel
for observation of decompression times.
Special Oyster case with shoulders
protecting the Triplock winding crown,
waterproof to 300 m/1,000 feet.
Selfwinding.
Sapphire crystal.

Ref. 17013
Oysterquartz DATEJUST,
chronometer in steel and gold.
Integral bracelet.
Waterproof to 100 m/330 feet.
Sapphire crystal.

Ref. 17014
Oysterquartz DATEJUST,
chronometer in steel with
white gold bezel.
Steel intergral bracelet.
Waterproof to 100 m/330 feet.
Sapphire crystal.

Ref. 18028
Oyster Perpetual
DAY-DATE, chronometer in 18 ct gold.
President bracelet.
Waterproof to 100 m/330 feet.
Selfwinding.
Sapphire crystal.
Weekday available in all major languages.

Ref. 18038
Oyster Perpetual
DAY-DATE, chronometer in 18 ct gold.
President bracelet.
Waterproof to 100 m/330 feet.
Selfwinding.
Sapphire crystal.
Weekday available in all major languages.

  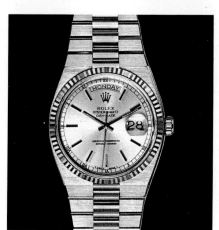

Ref. 18039 Bicolore
Oyster Perpetual
DAY-DATE, chronometer
in 18 ct white gold, yellow gold bezel.
TRIDOR bracelet with pink/yellow/
white gold centre links.
Waterproof to 100 m/330 feet.
Selfwinding.
Sapphire crystal.
Weekday available in all major languages.

Ref. 18046
Oyster Perpetual
DAY-DATE, chronometer in platinum.
President bracelet.
Bezel and dial set with brilliants.
Waterproof to 100 m/330 feet.
Selfwinding.
Sapphire crystal.
Weekday available in all major languages.

Ref. 18078
Oyster Perpetual
DAY-DATE, chronometer in 18 ct gold
with "bark" finish.
Matching President bracelet.
Waterproof to 100 m/330 feet.
Selfwinding.
Sapphire crystal.
Weekday available in all major languages.

Ref. 18168
Oyster Perpetual
DAY-DATE, chronometer in 18 ct gold.
President bracelet.
Bezel set with 24 baguettes.
Waterproof to 100 m/330 feet.
Selfwinding.
Sapphire crystal.
Weekday available in all major languages.

Ref. 19018
Oysterquartz DAY-DATE,
chronometer in 18 ct gold.
Integral bracelet.
Waterproof to 100 m/330 feet.
Sapphire crystal.
Weekday available in all major languages.

Ref. 19019
Oysterquartz DAY-DATE,
chronometer in 18 ct gold.
Integral bracelet.
Waterproof to 100 m/330 feet.
Sapphire crystal.
Weekday available in all major languages.

  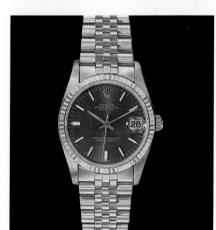

Ref. 19028
Oysterquartz DAY-DATE,
chronometer in 18 ct gold
with "pyramid" finish.
Matching integral bracelet.
Waterproof to 100 m/330 feet.
Sapphire crystal.
Weekday available in all major languages.

Ref. 19048
Oysterquartz DAY-DATE,
chronometer in 18 ct gold.
Integral bracelet.
Bezel and dial set with brilliants.
Waterproof to 100 m/330 feet.
Sapphire crystal.
Weekday available in all major languages.

Ref. 67188
Lady
OYSTER PERPETUAL
in 18 ct gold.
Oyster bracelet.
Waterproof to 100 m/330 feet.
Selfwinding.
Sapphire crystal.

Ref. 67193
Lady
OYSTER PERPETUAL
in steel and gold.
Oyster bracelet.
Waterproof to 100 m/330 feet.
Selfwinding.
Sapphire crystal.

Ref. 68240
Oyster Perpetual
DATEJUST,
chronometer in steel.
Jubilee bracelet.
Waterproof to 100 m/330 feet.
Selfwinding.
Sapphire crystal.

Ref. 68273
Oyster Perpetual
DATEJUST,
chronometer in steel and gold.
Jubilee bracelet.
Waterproof to 100 m/330 feet.
Selfwinding.
Sapphire crystal.

 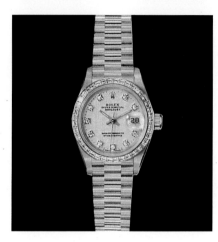 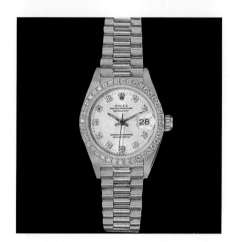

Ref. 68278
Oyster Perpetual
DATEJUST,
chronometer in 18 ct gold.
Jubilee bracelet.
Waterproof to 100 m/330 feet.
Selfwinding.
Sapphire crystal.

Ref. 68279 Bicolore
Oyster Perpetual
DATEJUST,
chronometer in 18 ct white gold,
yellow gold bezel.
TRIDOR bracelet with
pink/yellow/white gold centre links.
Waterproof to 100 m/330 feet.
Selfwinding.
Sapphire crystal.

Ref. 69018
Oyster Perpetual
Lady DATEJUST,
chronometer in 18 ct gold with
engraved bezel.
Matching Jubilee bracelet.
Waterproof to 100 m/330 feet.
Selfwinding.
Sapphire crystal.

Ref. 69068
Oyster Perpetual
Lady DATEJUST,
chronometer in 18 ct gold.
President bracelet.
Bezel set with brilliants and
4 baguette rubies.
Dial set with 10 brilliants.
Waterproof to 100 m/330 feet.
Selfwinding.
Sapphire crystal.

Ref. 69128
Oyster Perpetual
Lady DATEJUST,
chronometer in 18 ct gold.
President bracelet.
Bezel set with 40 baguettes.
Dial set with brilliants.
Waterproof to 100 m/330 feet.
Selfwinding.
Sapphire crystal.

Ref. 69138
Oyster Perpetual
Lady DATEJUST,
chronometer in 18 ct gold.
President bracelet.
Bezel and dial set with brilliants.
Waterproof to 100 m/330 feet.
Selfwinding.
Sapphire crystal.

  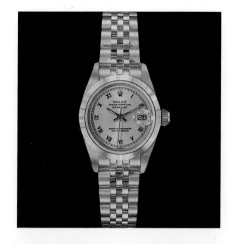

 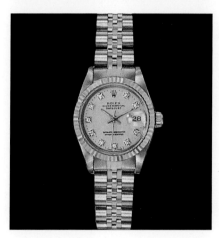 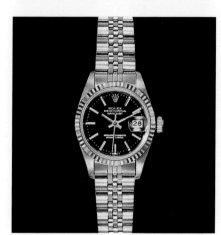

Ref. 69160
Oyster Perpetual
Lady DATE in steel.
Jubilee bracelet.
Waterproof to 100 m/330 feet.
Selfwinding.
Sapphire crystal.

Ref. 69163
Oyster Perpetual
Lady DATEJUST,
chronometer in steel and gold.
Jubilee bracelet.
Waterproof to 100 m/330 feet.
Selfwinding.
Sapphire crystal.

Ref. 69168
Oyster Perpetual
Lady DATEJUST,
chronometer in 18 ct gold.
Jubilee bracelet.
Waterproof to 100 m/330 feet.
Selfwinding.
Sapphire crystal.

Ref. 69173
Oyster Perpetual
Lady DATEJUST,
chronometer in steel and gold.
Jubilee bracelet.
Dial set with brilliants.
Waterproof to 100 m/330 feet.
Selfwinding.
Sapphire crystal.

Ref. 69173
Oyster Perpetual
Lady DATEJUST,
Chronometer in steel and gold.
Jubilee bracelet.
Waterproof to 100 m/330 feet.
Selfwinding.
Sapphire crystal.

Ref. 69174
Oyster Perpetual
Lady DATEJUST,
chronometer in steel
with white gold bezel.
Steel Jubilee bracelet.
Waterproof to 100 m 330 feet.
Selfwinding.
Sapphire crystal.

  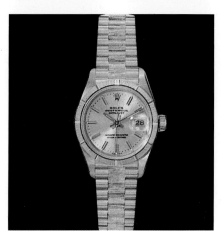

Ref. 69178
Oyster Perpetual
Lady DATEJUST,
chronometer in 18 ct gold.
President bracelet.
Waterproof to 100 m/330 feet.
Selfwinding.
Sapphire crystal.

Ref. 69179
Oyster Perpetual
Lady DATEJUST,
chronometer in 18 ct gold.
President bracelet.
Waterproof to 100 m/330 feet.
Selfwinding.
Sapphire crystal.

Ref. 69179 Bicolore
Oyster Perpetual
Lady DATEJUST,
chronometer in 18 ct white gold,
yellow gold bezel.
TRIDOR bracelet with pink/yellow/
white gold centre links.
Waterproof to 100 m/330 feet.
Selfwinding.
Sapphire crystal.

Ref. 69190
Oyster Perpetual
Lady DATE in steel.
Oyster bracelet.
Waterproof to 100 m/330 feet.
Selfwinding.
Sapphire crystal.

Ref. 69198 SAPH
Oyster Perpetual
Lady DATEJUST,
chronometer in 18 ct gold.
Jubilee bracelet.
Bezel set with sapphires and brilliants.
Dial set with 10 brilliants.
Waterproof to 100 m/330 feet.
Selfwinding.
Sapphire crystal.

Ref. 69278
Oyster Perpetual
Lady DATEJUST,
chronometer in 18 ct gold with "bark" finish.
Matching President bracelet.
Waterproof to 100 m/330 feet.
Selfwinding.
Sapphire crystal.

DIALS, CASES AND MOVEMENTS

EBAUCHES S.A.
NEUCHATEL
SUISSE

VALJOUX S. A.
LES BIOUX

13''' **VZ 23**
29,5 mm

Chronographe-compteur à 2 poussoirs, avec roue à colonnes

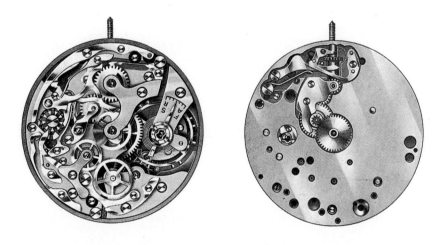

Mouvement agrandi

COMMUNICATION TECHNIQUE ET PRATIQUE A L'USAGE DE L'HORLOGER-RHABILLEUR

2

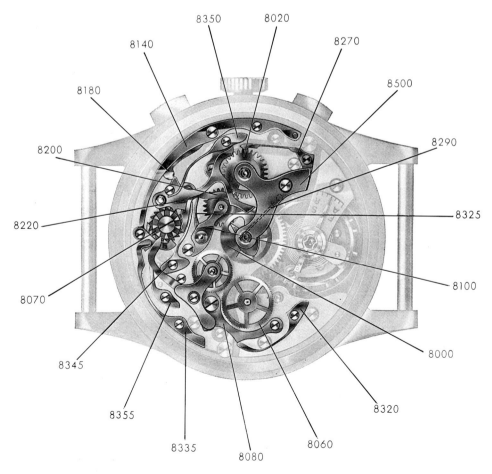

Ebauches S. A., Neuchâtel, Suisse

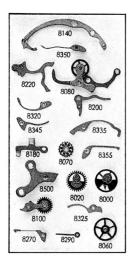

DÉMONTAGE :

1. Désarmer le ressort de barillet en agissant sur le cliquet indiqué par la flèche.
2. Enlever le balancier et l'ancre.
3. Sortir la tige de remontoir.
4. Sortir le poussoir de commande s'il est à rainure sans oublier de soulever la commande 8140 dont le plot est engagé dans la rainure du pivot du poussoir, puis extraire le mouvement. Si le poussoir de commande est à ressort ou à oreille, extraire le mouvement puis les poussoirs. Ensuite dans les 2 cas, enlever les aiguilles et le cadran.
5. Enlever le ressort du marteau 8350 et le marteau monté 8220.
6. Enlever l'embrayage monté 8080 et son ressort 8320.
7. Enlever le bloqueur 8200 et son ressort 8345.
8. Enlever la commande montée 8140, son ressort 8335 et la bascule de remise à zéro 8180.
9. Enlever la roue à colonnes 8070 et son sautoir 8355.
10. Enlever le pont de chronographe 8500, le mobile de compteur 8020 et le mobile de chronographe 8000.
11. Enlever le baladeur monté 8100 et son ressort 8325.
12. Enlever le sautoir du compteur de minutes 8270, le ressort-friction 8290 et la roue entraîneuse 8060 ; cette dernière à l'aide d'un levier en forme de fourchette.
13. Démonter le mouvement et nettoyer toutes les pièces selon le procédé habituel.

CONTROLE A :

Contrôler l'état du doigt et des dents du mobile de chronographe, de la roue d'embrayage et de la roue entraîneuse. Retirer le pont de la roue d'embrayage, nettoyer les bouchons de cette dernière et vérifier qu'elle soit libre. Procéder de même pour la roue du baladeur si nécessaire. Nettoyer également le tube de la roue de centre et vérifier que le bouchon intérieur soit en place.
Remonter la partie montre ; huiler tous les mobiles et armer le ressort d'un tour et demi pour contrôler la marche. Avant le remontage du mécanisme chronographe, il est recommandé d'enlever le balancier et l'ancre.

REMONTAGE :

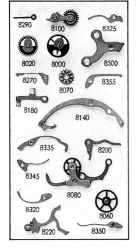

1. Visser le ressort-friction 8290.
2. Poser le baladeur monté 8100 et son ressort 8325 (le baladeur doit être libre).
3. Remettre le mobile de compteur 8020, le mobile de chronographe 8000 après avoir huilé son long pivot (vérifier que la pression du ressort-friction 8290 s'exerce normalement sous le mobile 8000) puis remettre le pont de chronographe 8500.
4. Visser le sautoir du compteur de minutes 8270 ; vérifier qu'il soit légèrement tendu.
5. Placer la roue à colonnes 8070 après avoir graissé la vis puis poser son sautoir 8355.
6. Poser la bascule de remise à zéro 8180 puis la commande montée 8140 et son ressort 8335.
7. Visser le bloqueur 8200 et son ressort 8345.
8. Huiler le pivot court du mobile de chronographe 8000 et les 2 pivots de la roue d'embrayage ; poser ensuite l'embrayage monté 8080 avec sa vis et visser le ressort d'embrayage 8320 (il ne faut jamais huiler les pivots du mobile de compteur et de la roue du baladeur).
9. Placer la roue entraîneuse 8060 ; elle doit être au même niveau que la roue d'embrayage.
10. Poser le marteau monté 8220 et son ressort 8350.
11. Vérifier la totale liberté de tous les mobiles puis remettre en place l'ancre et le balancier.

CONTROLE B :

Contrôler les pénétrations d'engrenages : roue entraîneuse - roue d'embrayage ; roue d'embrayage - roue chronographe ; passage du doigt dans la denture de la roue du baladeur.
En opérant la remise à zéro par l'appui du marteau sur les cœurs, vérifier que le mobile de chronographe soit bloqué ; par contre le mobile de compteur doit avoir un très léger jeu (le marteau n'appuie pas sur le cœur). Vérifier également que la roue du baladeur soit éloignée du doigt, que les bras du marteau ne touchent ni aux roues, ni au pont et que la roue à colonnes maintienne désaccouplée la roue d'embrayage de la roue de chronographe. Lors d'une pression sur le poussoir de remise à zéro, vérifier qu'au début du déplacement le bec du marteau s'arc-boute contre la goupille du bloqueur, puis la pression augmentant, le déclenchement de la remise à zéro s'opère. Graisser légèrement le marteau aux points de contact avec les cœurs, avec le baladeur et avec la goupille du bloqueur ; la bascule d'embrayage au point de contact avec la roue à colonnes ; le bloqueur au point de contact avec la roue à colonnes ; le ressort de commande au point de contact avec le cliquet de commande ; le sautoir de roue à colonnes au point de contact avec la denture de la roue à colonnes.

EMBOITAGE :

Les poussoirs à ressort ou à oreille doivent être mis en place avant l'emboîtage. Par contre les poussoirs à rainure doivent être mis en place après l'emboîtage, en dévissant la commande, éventuellement la bascule de remise à zéro. Ensuite dans les 2 cas, remettre la tige de remontoir, poser les 2 vis de fixage puis contrôler le fonctionnement par les poussoirs. Placer le cadran et les aiguilles d'heure, de minute et de seconde, puis le marteau étant maintenu sur les cœurs par le poussoir de remise à zéro, poser l'aiguille de seconde au centre puis l'aiguille de compteur.

Remarque : Ce mouvement à 2 poussoirs a été également construit avec 1 poussoir (3 fonctions). Les pièces ci-dessous dont le numéro est complété par /1 sont particulières au mécanisme à 1 poussoir. La commande 8140¹/1 est utilisée dans l'exécution avec poussoir dans la couronne de remontoir.

Description et numérotation des pièces de rechange d'après le « Dictionnaire Technologique des Parties de la Montre » 2ᵐᵉ édition.

100	Platine	420	Roue de couronne	8080	Embrayage monté
106	Pont de barillet et de rouage	423	Noyau de roue de couronne	8100	Baladeur monté, 30m
118	Pont combiné	425	Cliquet	8102	Tenon du baladeur
121	Coq pour spiral plat	430	Ressort de cliquet	8140	Commande montée
125	Pont d'ancre	435	Bascule	8180	Bascule de remise à zéro
182	Barillet avec couvercle	440	Ressort de bascule	8200	Bloqueur
195	Arbre de barillet	443	Tirette	8220	Marteau monté
206	Roue de centre	445	Ressort de tirette	8221	Tenon de marteau
210	Roue moyenne	450	Renvoi	8270	Sautoir du compteur de minutes
225	Roue de seconde	453	Renvoi intermédiaire	8290	Ressort-friction
245	Chaussée	466	Couvre-mécanisme	8320	Ressort d'embrayage
255	Roue des heures	705	Roue d'ancre pivotée	8325	Ressort du baladeur
260	Roue de minuterie	710	Ancre montée	8335	Ressort de commande
301	Raquette pour spiral plat	714	Tige d'ancre	8345	Ressort du bloqueur
311	Coqueret empierré	721	Balancier avec spiral plat	8350	Ressort du marteau
330	Plaque de contre-pivot pour balancier	723	Axe de balancier	8355	Sautoir de roue à colonnes
401	Tige de remontoir	730	Plateau	8400	Excentrique de pivotement d'embrayage
407	Pignon coulant	8000	Mobile de chronographe monté	8401	Excentrique-appui d'embrayage
410	Pignon de remontoir	8020	Mobile monté du compteur de minutes, 30m	8406	Excentrique de pénétration du doigt
415	Rochet	8060	Roue entraîneuse	8500	Pont de chronographe
		8070	Roue à colonnes		

5101 Vis de fixage - 5106 Vis de pont de barillet et de rouage, tête haute - 5106¹ Vis de pont de barillet et de rouage, tête basse - 5118 Vis de pont combiné - 5121 Vis de coq - 5125 Vis de pont d'ancre - 5311 Vis de coqueret - 5330 Vis de plaque de contre-pivot - 5423 Vis de noyau de roue de couronne - 5425 Vis de cliquet - 5430 Vis de ressort de cliquet - 5435 Vis de bascule - 5440 Vis de ressort de bascule - 5443 Vis de tirette - 5445 Vis de ressort de tirette - 5466 Vis de couvre-mécanisme - 5738 Vis de piton - 5751 Clef de cadran - 58070 Vis de roue à colonnes - 58080 Vis d'embrayage - 58140 Vis de commande - 58200 Vis de bloqueur - 58270 Vis de sautoir du compteur de minutes - 58290 Vis du ressort-friction - 58320 Vis de ressort d'embrayage - 58325 Vis de ressort de baladeur - 58335 Vis de ressort de commande - 58345 Vis de ressort de bloqueur - 58350 Vis de ressort de marteau - 58355 Vis de sautoir de roue à colonnes - 58500 Vis de pont de chronographe.

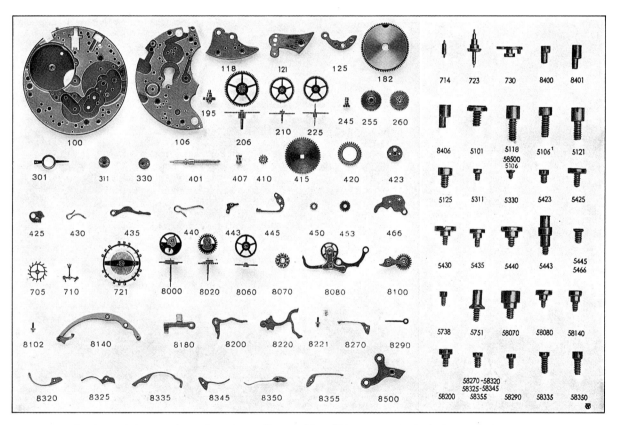

Par suite d'améliorations techniques, quelques pièces de ce calibre ont été modifiées au cours des fabrications successives. Il y a de ce fait plusieurs exécutions; pour différencier entre elles celles qui ne sont pas interchangeables, une lettre a été ajoutée au numéro de base de ces pièces. L'usage de signes spéciaux accompagnant certains numéros de pièces donne de précisions à ce sujet. Avec *: aucune interchangeabilité. Si le numéro est entre parenthèses, la pièce qu'il représente ne se fabrique plus. De plus, il existe des pièces d'ancienne exécution dont la forme est différente de celle des pièces représentées sur cette communication technique ; elles n'y figurent pas étant donné leur complète interchangeabilité.

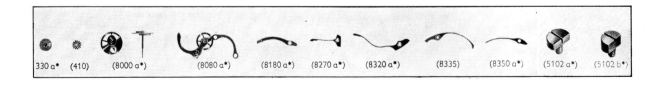

330 a*   (410)   (8000 a*)   (8080 a*)   (8180 a*)   (8270 a*)   (8320 a*)   (8335)   (8350 a*)   (5102 a*)   (5102 b*)

Lors de la commande d'une pièce pour un dispositif amortisseur, veuillez préciser le genre de ce dernier. D'autre part, pour de plus amples détails sur la désignation et la numérotation des fournitures de rechange, veuillez consulter le « Dictionnaire Technologique des Parties de la Montre », 2ᵐᵉ édition, publié par Ebauches S. A.

Indiquez à votre fournituriste le numéro et la désignation des pièces que vous désirez et vous serez rapidement satisfaits.

Paul Attinger S. A., Neuchâtel

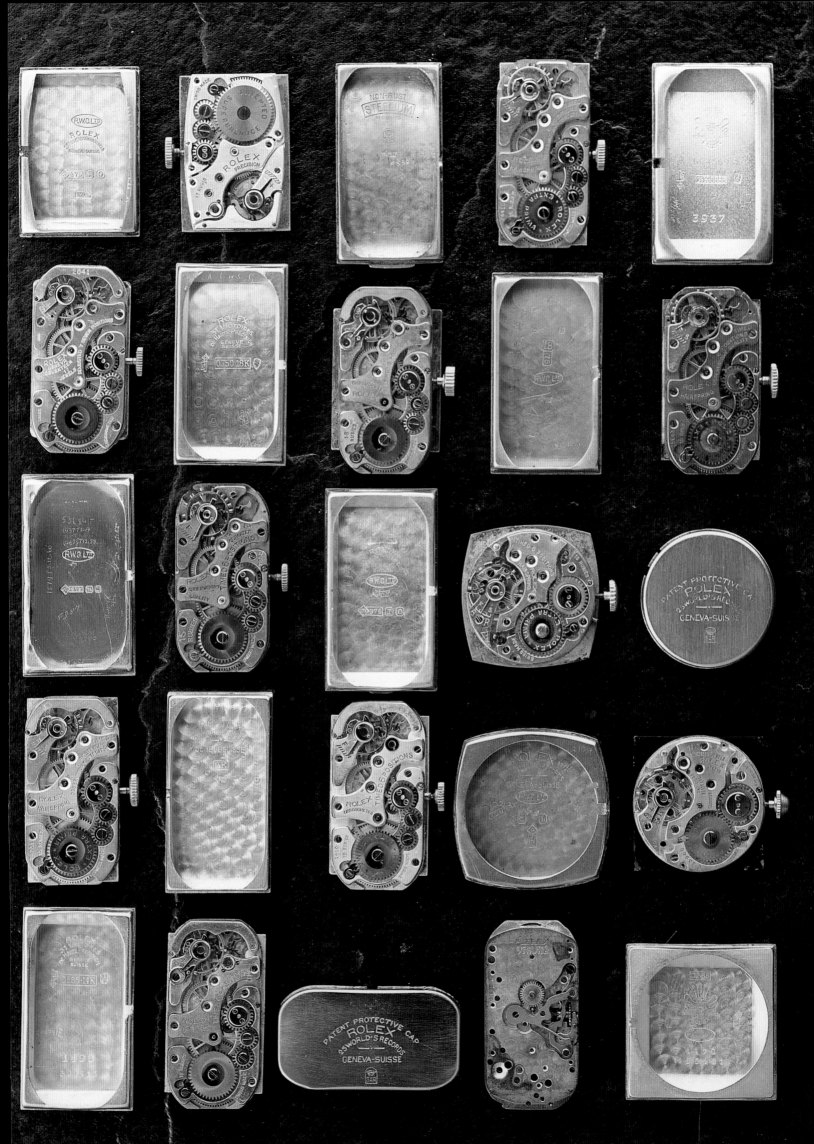

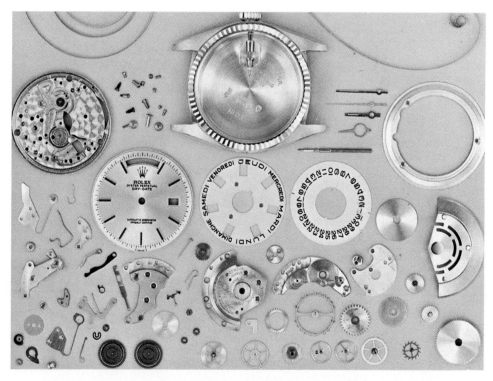

A harmony of more than 220 separate pieces, some of them incredibly tiny.
All these parts are contained within a diameter of 28.5 millimetres (1.122")
and a height of 5.6 millimetres (0.22") and tolerances are usually measured
in microns (thousandths of a millimetre).
The Day-Date combines all the features invented or perfected by
Rolex—swimproof Oyster case, Perpetual rotor self-winding mechanism,
superlative chronometer movement and date and day of the week written out in full.
Possibly the most brilliant timepiece in the world today and available
only in 18 ct. gold or platinum.

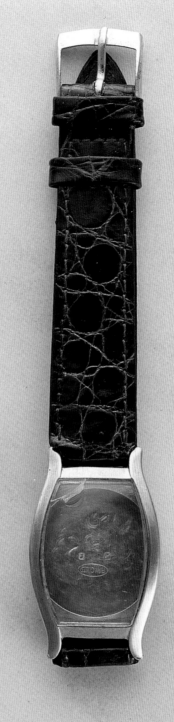

TIMELESS ELEGANCE

ORIGINAL DESIGNS OF ROLEX

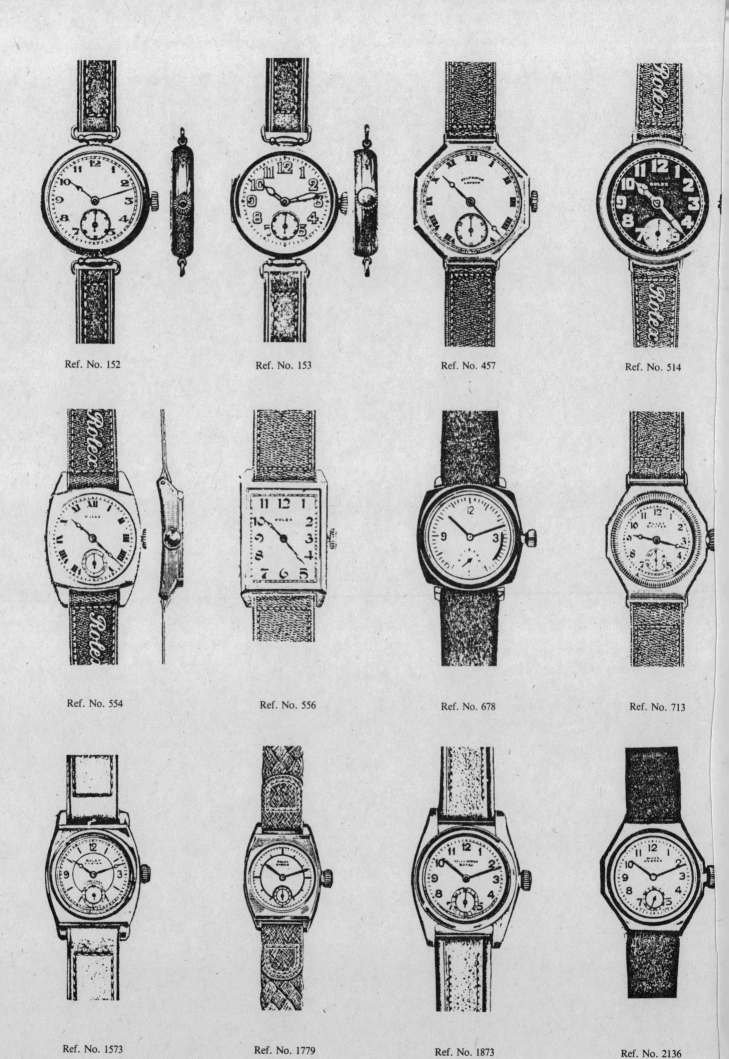

Ref. No. 152   Ref. No. 153   Ref. No. 457   Ref. No. 514

Ref. No. 554   Ref. No. 556   Ref. No. 678   Ref. No. 713

Ref. No. 1573   Ref. No. 1779   Ref. No. 1873   Ref. No. 2136

Ref. No. 515

Ref. No. 537

Ref. No. 540

Ref. No. 545

Ref. No. 714

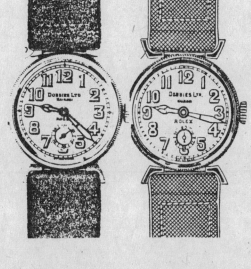
Ref. No. 753M

Ref. No. 753

Ref. No. 756

Ref. No. 2081

Ref. No. 2081

Ref. No. 2190

Ref. No. 2227

Ref. No. 546

Ref. No. 547

Ref. No. 548

Ref. No. 549

Ref. No. 930

Ref. No. 931

Ref. No. 1195

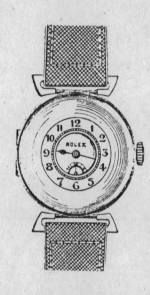

Ref. No. 1237

Ref. No. 2233

Ref. No. 2295

Ref. No. 2296

Ref. No. 2303

Ref. No. 2323

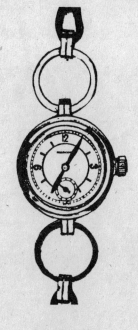

Ref. No. 2324

Ref. No. 2332

Ref. No. 2515

Ref. No. 2532

Ref. No. 2574

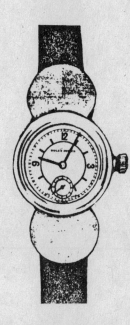

Ref. No. 2590

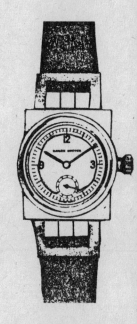

Ref. No. 2593

Ref. No. 2916

Ref. No. 2917

Ref. No. 2940

Ref. No. 2942

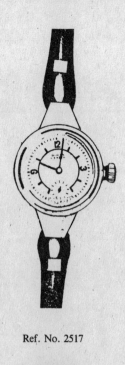

Ref. No. 2517

Ref. No. 2518

Ref. No. 2524

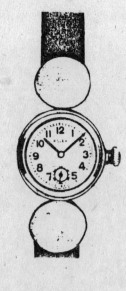

Ref. No. 2528

Ref. No. 2595

Ref. No. 2595

Ref. No. 2705

Ref. No. 2764

Ref. No. 3009

Ref. No. 3039

Ref. No. 3064

Ref. No. 3065

Ref. No. 2529

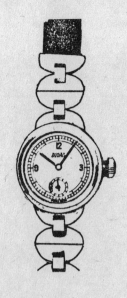

Ref. No. 2530

Ref. No. 2533

Ref. No. 2765

Ref. No. 2784

Ref. No. 2803

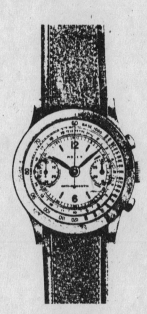

Ref. No. 2811

Ref. No. 3082

Ref. No. 3096

Ref. No. 3116

Ref. No. 3121

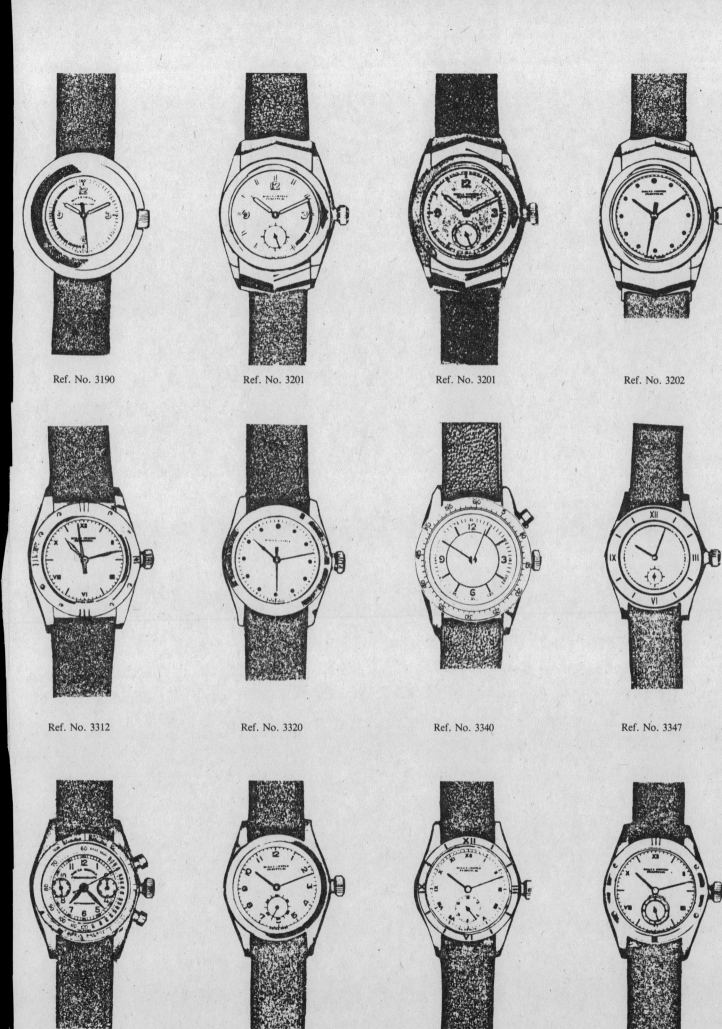

Ref. No. 3190   Ref. No. 3201   Ref. No. 3201   Ref. No. 3202

Ref. No. 3312   Ref. No. 3320   Ref. No. 3340   Ref. No. 3347

Ref. No. 3481 L.G.   Ref. No. 3483   Ref. No. 3490   Ref. No. 3495 L.G.

Ref. No. 3159

Ref. No. 3172

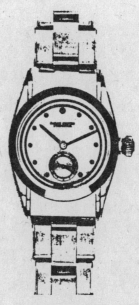

Ref. No. 3172 F

Ref. No. 3189

Ref. No. 3241

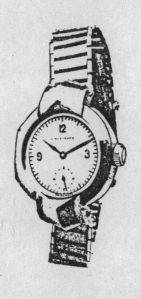

Ref. No. 3242

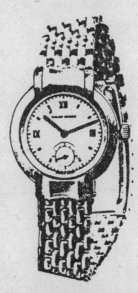

Ref. No. 3263

Ref. No. 3311

Ref. No. 3372

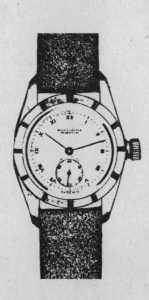

Ref. No. 3458 L.A.

Ref. No. 3479

Ref. No. 3481

Ref. No. 3134

Ref. No. 3135

Ref. No. 3136

Ref. No. 3139

Ref. No. 3203

Ref. No. 3204

Ref. No. 3205

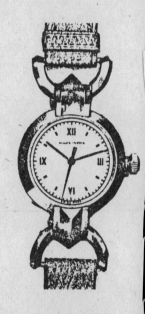

Ref. No. 3206

Ref. No. 3353

Ref. No. 3355

Ref. No. 3359

Ref. No. 3370

Ref. No. 3506   Ref. No. 3525   Ref. No. 3536   Ref. No. 3548

Ref. No. 3597   Ref. No. 3598   Ref. No. 3599   Ref. No. 3604 L.G.

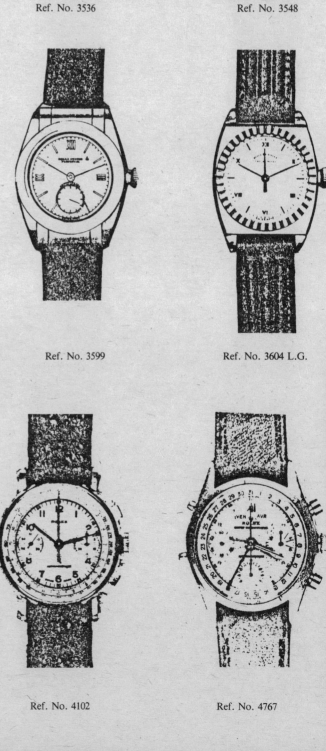

Ref. No. 3835   Ref. No. 4100   Ref. No. 4102   Ref. No. 4767

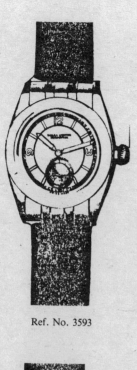

Ref. No. 3593

Ref. No. 3594

Ref. No. 3595c.

Ref. No. 801

Ref. No. 3616

Ref. No. 3668

Ref. No. 3761

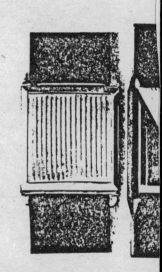

Ref. No. 977   Ref.

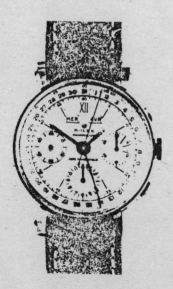

Ref. No. 4768

Ref. No. 8124

Ref. No. 8206

Ref. No. 2314

Ref. No. 813

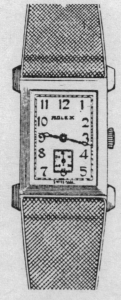

Ref. No. 868

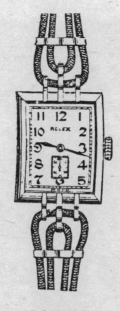

Ref. No. 869

Ref. No. 871

No. 977

Ref. No. 1785/2850

Ref. No. 1835/2846

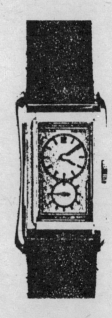

Ref. No. 1855

Ref. No. 2315

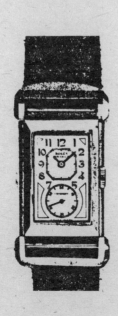

Ref. No. 2539

Ref. No. 2540

Ref. No. 2541

Ref. No. 961

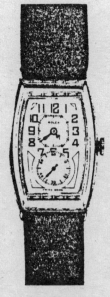

Ref. No. 962

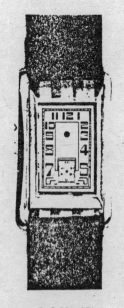

Ref. No. 971

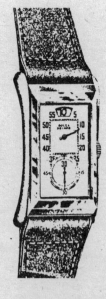

Ref. No. 1491

Ref. No. 1863/2847

Ref. No. 2149

Ref. No. 2150

Ref. No. 2313

Ref. No. 2660

Ref. No. 2661

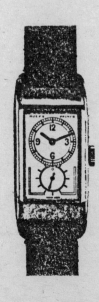

Ref. No. 2879

Ref. No. 3275

TIMELESS ELEGANCE

EST

Since 1919, the Gold family have been purveyors of fine watches in Los Angeles. Seventy years later, Bradley Gold continues the family tradition at the L.A. WATCH CO. The L.A. WATCH CO. is committed to the collector of vintage and investment timepieces, backed by a lifetime of knowledge and expertise. At L.A. WATCH CO., watches are more than just a hobby, they're our life. Featuring the largest selection of fine vintage Rolex anywhere in North America.

最高級ヴィンテージ ローレックスを北アメリカ でどこよりも一番取揃えています。

VINTAGE

No.7 Piccadilly Arcade,
— OPPOSITE the ROYAL ACADEMY —
Watches, – Clocks, – Tools, – Books & Items of Horological Interest
London S.W.1.
01-499 6526

FINEST COLLECTION OF ANTIQUE POCKET WATCHES
AND WRIST WATCHES IN LONDON
FOR THE COLLECTOR

Somlo Antiques

From the Renaissance...to the wristwatch
Experience and Expertise

PRECISION - SKILL - ROLEX

SIMPLY SPECTACULAR JEWELRY

12.02.ct. COGNAC DIAMOND
G.I.A. CERTIFICATE

Subject to priorsale

THE BRONSON COLLECTION
at
BOOGIES

534 E. COOPER ST.   303-925-6111
ASPEN COLORADO 81611   IN SEASON OR BY APPT.
U.S.A.

Buyers and Sellers of Rare Jewellery and Watches

The Chancery Bullion Company is one of the leading dealers in rare and interesting jewellery and watches. If you wish to buy or sell, The Chancery Bullion Company guarantees a genuine service and the most competitive prices.

15 Greville Street,
London EC1N 8SQ

Tel : 01-831 3096
Fax: 01-430 2345

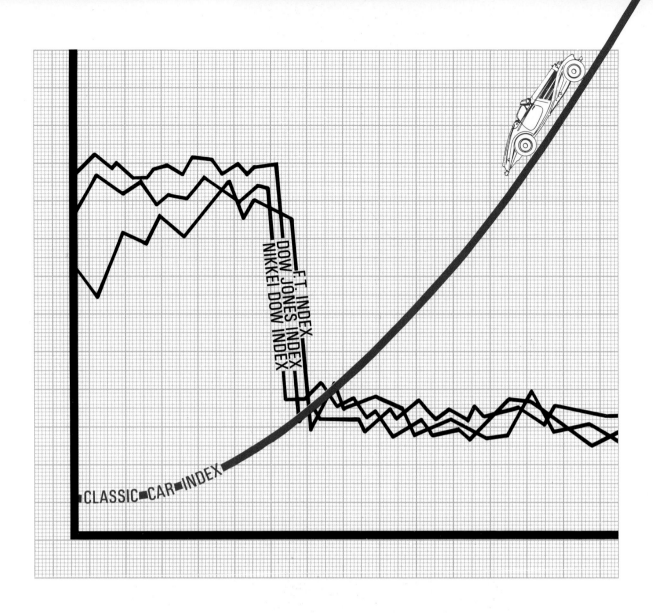

The chart labels read: F.T. INDEX, DOW JONES INDEX, NIKKEI DOW INDEX, CLASSIC CAR INDEX

CHRISTOPHER RENWICK LTD.
PURVEYOR OF THE FINEST CARS IN THE WORLD

PURCHASERS AND SELLERS ON BEHALF OF PRIVATE COLLECTORS, INSTITUTIONS AND MUSEUMS.

21 BROOK MEWS NORTH, LONDON W2 3BW
TELEPHONE: 01·402 2447 FAX 01·402 8859

FOR YOUR COLLECTION

If you are interested in other books about wristwatches, we have a large selection to choose from.
Please contact us with what you are looking for and we will be happy to locate it for you.

We have the following titles in stock:

A. *Master of Time*   @US$150.00
B. *Patek Philippe*   @US$190.00
C. *Wrist Watches*   @US$ 75.00
D. *American Wristwatch — 5 Decades of Design AND Style*   @US$ 90.00

Fill in the form and return it to Dragon print International Ltd.
18/F JAVA CENTRE, 128 JAVA ROAD, NORTH POINT, HONG KONG.

I would like to order the following books.

Title	Unit Cost	Quantity	Total Cost
A	US$150.00		
B	US$190.00		
C	US$ 75.00		
D	US$ 90.00		
		TOTAL :	

Other titles that are not on the list:

_____

Please add postal charge of US$15 for air shipment outside H.K.

NAME   : _____   ☐ Cheque enclosed
            _____   (payable to Dragonprint International Ltd.)

ADDRESS : _____   ☐ Charge my credit card
            _____   ☐ American Express
            _____   ☐ Visa
            _____   Card No. _____
            _____   Expiry _____
TEL   : _____   Signature _____